Enjoying Health &
Longevity With
Nutritional Immunology

Contents

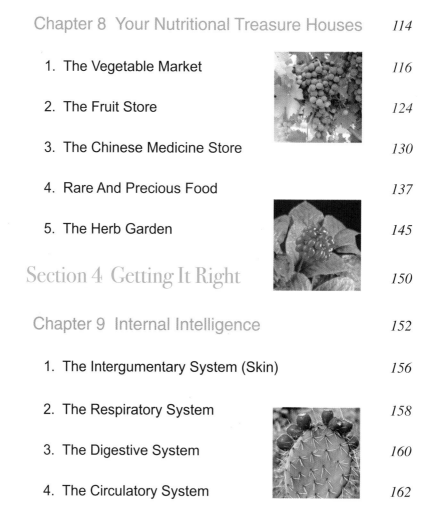

Section 1

Our Immune System —
The Best Doctor In The World

Most illnesses are caused by a malfunctioning immune system

Nutritional Immunology & A Healthy Life

Chapter 1 The Human Immune System

Each of us is born with the best doctor in the world—our immune system. A healthy and well-cared for immune system effectively prevents most illnesses.

Nutritional Immunology is a science that studies the link between nutrition and the immune system. According to Nutritional Immunology, nutrient-rich foods contribute to a strong immune response, which in turn neutralizes disease-causing germs and prevents infections. Similarly, when we are ill, such foods will help us to recover faster. Many take extra effort to eat nutritiously when sick, but few take precautions that could have prevented the illness altogether.

Nutritional Immunology focuses on caring for overall health and acts as preventive maintenance against diseases. Its message is simple—by preventing diseases, we don't have to worry about curing them. Think of it as similar to fighting a raging fire. It is best and easiest to control the flames before they grow.

1. A Proactive Defender

The immune system is an amazing, proactive defense mechanism. Its complex network of white blood cells, antibodies and other immune chemicals and organs offers us around-the-clock protection against invaders. When there is a cut on the skin, the immune system works actively to heal it and stop the entry of microbes like viruses and bacteria. As our cells continuously reproduce, a strong immune system also helps to detect and defeat cell mutations that could lead to cancer.

Most diseases are the result of a malfunctioning immune system. The immune system may malfunction in one or both of the following ways:

A Weak Immune System

You may have come across someone who constantly gets sick — be it with flu, a cough, cold or even stomach discomfort. Have you ever wondered why some people recover quickly while others

take longer or just never fully recover? The answer lies in our immune system.

The air we breathe, the food we eat and the surfaces we touch are always teeming with disease-causing dust, pollutants, fungi,parasites and germs like viruses and bacteria. Once our body is weak, these toxic agents will easily overwhelm the immune system and cause illnesses.

Acquired Immune Deficiency Syndrome (AIDS) is one example of a disease linked with a weak immune system. Once AIDS sets in, the immune system is critically compromised and unable to effectively combat dangerous germs. Cancer is also a sign that our immune system is weak. Chemotherapy, a type of radiation treatment for cancer, further weakens the immune system—this is why cancer patients are easily afflicted with flu, coughs and colds.

A Hyperactive Immune System

The immune system can also malfunction by over-reacting or turning against the body's own cells. This often leads to allergies or autoimmune diseases.

An allergic reaction, such as a respiratory allergy, skin allergy or food allergy, occurs when the immune system reacts against non-threatening agents, such as plant pollen, animal fur, dust and some types of food.

An autoimmune disease occurs when our immune system mistakenly attacks our body's own healthy cells. Rheumatoid arthritis, multiple sclerosis, psoriasis, diabetes mellitus and systemic lupus erythematosus are all examples of common autoimmune diseases.

Doctors treat allergies and autoimmune diseases by prescribing drugs to suppress the immune response. Such treatment usually results in a weakened immune system, thus, leaving us more susceptible to diseases. And usually, such drugs only stop the symptoms, such as swelling or pain. They do not completely cure the disease. In addition, medications result in a wide array of harmful side effects.

A Balanced System Is Best

Inside our body is an exquisitely crafted immune system. Most of the time, we will not even be aware that it is continuously working, albeit silently, in the background!

For the majority of us, our immune system is neither over active or under active. We are therefore, blessed with a healthy and balanced defense mechanism that can successfully protect us from many diseases.

However, we must remember not to take the immune system for granted as a number of factors can undermine its effectiveness. Some of these factors include an unbalanced diet, stress, over-exertion, chemotherapy as well as the affects of aging and certain hereditary medical conditions.

2. A System Without Substitute

Diseases Do Not Occur Overnight

Many think that diseases pop up suddenly. Actually, we could have been infected long before a disease's symptoms are felt. Some germs reside in our bodies for years before symptoms are evident. The human immunodeficiency virus (HIV), which is responsible

for AIDS, is one example. An infected person could be carrying HIV for 10 years before the onset of AIDS.

Another example is cancer, which is not as easily detectable or diagnosed as the flu. In the vast majority of cases, cancer is only diagnosed a few years after its onset.

When we finally experience symptoms, our first reaction is to cure it immediately. Unfortunately, our immune system needs time to recover from an infection and strengthen its forces sufficiently to mount a victorious counter-attack.

In order for our immune system to win the fight, we must nourish it on a daily basis, rather than simply wait for an illness to strike before finding a solution. Again, only by proactively defending our body against infection can we avoid getting sick.

Limitations Of Drugs

The antibiotic is a commonly prescribed medication. It takes years of research and lots of researchers to test and perfect an antibiotic. But then, like most drugs, the antibiotic still has harmful side effects. In contrast, the myriad antibodies our immune system uses are completely safe and may be mass-produced very quickly.

It was only recently that experts realized just how much immune response contributes to a healthy and long life. Previously, it was common belief that doctors and drugs could cure almost any disease. But recent medical advances have shown that the human body works in complex ways and only the immune system can fight the threat of new, incurable diseases.

For example, before the rise of cancer and AIDS or new viral epidemics like Severe Acute Respiratory Syndrome (SARS), not much attention was given to the roles of Nutritional Immunology and the immune system in protecting the body.

There may be a small number of drugs that could help stimulate the immune system. However, the immune system involves a highly complicated interaction between millions of cells as well as chemicals and organs. These immune components know exactly how, when and where their action is needed to defeat invading substances without harming other cells of the body. Therefore, science would be hard-pressed to find a drug that could replace or replicate the immune system.

A clear example is when we have a cold. Cold medicine offers only short-term relief as the medicine only alleviates the symptoms. However, when we get good rest and have proper nutrition, the immune system regenerates and expels the virus quickly, bringing an end to our cold. It is once again clear that the most effective doctor in the world is the one that resides inside us!

A Balanced Diet, A Healthier Life

Infectious diseases were the main cause of death in ancient times. This was because living conditions then were less hygienic, putting mankind in closer proximity to higher quantities of harmful germs. Humans today enjoy more hygienic environments and a wealth of modern conveniences.

We may have conquered some of the most formidable diseases of our ancestors, but we are also stricken by new ones. This is compounded by our tendency to eat food that is high in fat, sugar, and salt and low in disease-preventing nutrients. Dietary imbalance in turn, imbalances the immune system leaving us more prone to illnesses like cancer, heart disease and a host of viral afflictions.

Although drugs can elicit certain responses from the immune system, they cannot replace its complex functions. Furthermore, these medications have side effects that can unsettle the immune system's delicate but highly effective balance.

Nutritional Immunology focuses on strengthening the immune system by eating wholesome plant foods. Such foods help us to proactively combat diseases without detrimental side effects. While learning more about the human immune system, scientists are also simultaneously discovering plant foods that are even more effective in bolstering immunity. These plant foods include mushrooms  like Shiitake, Maitake, Reishi, Agaricus Blazel Murill and Coriolus Versicolor. Such treasures of nature are said to both prevent cancer and enhance the vitality of the immune system.

17

Nutritional Immunology & A Healthy Life

Chapter 2 The Army Within

When it comes to security, few will question the need to invest billions of dollars in well-trained soldiers, sophisticated weaponry, around-the-clock surveillance and advanced back-up defenses. Similarly, each one of us is also equipped with an internal army that is as, if not more, efficient. The only difference is that its enemies are invisible to the naked eye.

The human body is constantly under threat from potentially dangerous and infectious microbes that are present all around us. These deadly invaders are ready and waiting to enter the body's various gateways and catch us off-guard.

Luckily, our body is protected by the state-of-the-art immune system. Our immune army never takes enemies for granted. An itching throat or tearing eyes are subtle signs that it is hard at work. Ironically, perhaps because we do not see it, we often ignore this army. We think about protecting our heart, skin and other organs but rarely consider the health of the immune system. Only when it is jeopardized and we fall ill do we even take notice.

1. Our Immune Battalions

The immune system is truly an amazing piece of work. At any given second, it can call upon a complex and concerted effort from countless different immune battalions. Their coordinated efforts work ceaselessly to protect us not only from external invaders but also from our own internal cells, which can mutate and become cancerous. Without the constant protection of our immune system, a simple dust particle could kill us!

Let us take a closer look at this army.

Our Body's Boot Camps: The Immune System

The immune system does not comprise one specific organ or location in the body. Instead, it involves several different organs, cells and chemicals working in well-oiled harmony.

Our skin is the first layer of defense. Unless cut, punctured, or otherwise

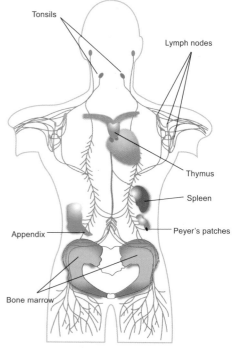

Tonsils

Lymph nodes

Thymus

Spleen

Peyer's patches

Appendix

Bone marrow

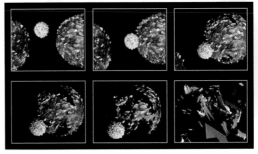

compromised, the skin protects us from invaders by secreting antibacterial substances like sweat, tears or sebum that trap and break down the cell walls of invaders.

How an NK cell destroys a cancer cell

Once the infiltrator goes past the skin and other initial defenses, other protectors roar into action. These include our lymphoid organs and white blood cells, which work together via a circulating system of lymph fluid and blood to kill invaders before they can reproduce.

Our major lymphoid organs are the thymus and bone marrow. These are supported by peripheral lymphoid organs like lymph nodes and the spleen. Recent studies indicate that two organs previously considered unnecessary, the appendix and tonsils, actually play important supporting roles within the immune system.

Red and white blood cells in a human blood stream. White blood cells are our immune cells

21

Soldier Factory: The Bone Marrow

The bone marrow creates red blood cells and white blood cells, the soldiers of the immune system. Every second, about eight million blood cells die and then the same number is regenerated.

Training Ground: The Thymus

Just as soldiers train for war with the navy, infantry or air force, the thymus assigns T cells their fighting duties. The thyms also secretes immune-regulating hormones.

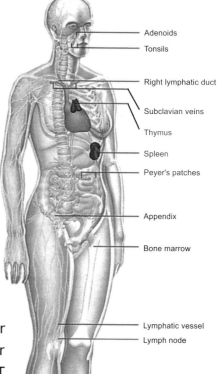

- Adenoids
- Tonsils
- Right lymphatic duct
- Subclavian veins
- Thymus
- Spleen
- Peyer's patches
- Appendix
- Bone marrow
- Lymphatic vessel
- Lymph node

Battlegrounds: The Lymph Nodes

Lymph nodes are little pockets of battlegrounds where billions of white blood cells gather, ready to wage war. While fighting infections, lymph nodes enlarge with foreign invaders and white blood cells to a point where you can actually feel the swelling. A swollen lymph node is a

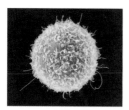

A human T cell

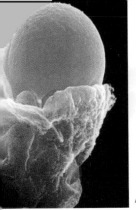

A macrophage engulfs an aged red blood cell

good indication that your immune system is hard at work against an infection. Lymph nodes also act as a drainage system — they filter the lymph fluid and carry away waste products like dead cells. The body contains about four times more lymph fluid than blood.

Blood Filter: The Spleen

The spleen is a blood reservoir that filters the blood to remove dead blood cells and engulfed viruses or bacteria. The spleen also signals B cells to produce large quantities of antibodies.

Throat Guards: The Tonsils

The tonsils constantly guard against invasion via the nose and mouth. People who have had their tonsils removed show a marked increase in getting Strep throat and Hodgkin's disease — indicating the importance of the tonsils in upper respiratory tract protection.

Immune Assistant: The Appendix

The appendix assists with B cell maturation and antibody (IgA) production. Additionally, the appendix coordinates traffic by producing molecules that direct white blood cells to other parts of the body. Another duty of the appendix is to guard the digestive tract and suppress potentially harmful antibody responses while promoting local immunity.

Intestinal Guards: Peyer's Patches

Like the appendix, Peyer's patches react to invaders in the intestines and are vital to the control of germs in our food.

The Body's Trusty Foot Soldiers

Our body's immune soldiers are the white blood cells. They consist primarily of B cells, T cells, phagocytes and granulocytes.

Specific Fighters: B Cells & Antibodies

B cells provide humeral immunity — protection via antibodies that circulate in our bodily fluids such as serum and the lymph. B cells fight invaders by producing antibodies specific to those invaders. Also known as immunoglobulins, antibodies are our enemy-seeking missiles that track and lock onto assigned invaders before triggering immune responses to destroy them.

Some B cells become "memory" cells. If the same invader attacks again, the memory B cells will identify and dispatch specific antibodies to defeat it.

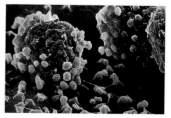

B cells produce over ten billion antibodies to fight various types of deadly pathogens

Non-Specific Fighters: T Cells

T cells give the body cellular immunity. They give non-specific immunity by seeking and destroying enemies regardless of type. Helper T cells command the immune system by rousing and issuing orders to other soldiers via chemical messengers. Cytotoxic T cells and NK cells are lethal snipers who shoot holes into invaders. Once the infection is controlled, suppressor T cells regulate antibody production and call an end to the war.

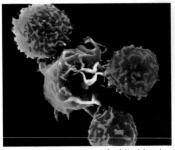

There are two groups of white blood cells: B cells that are made in the bone marrow and T cells that are trained in the thymus

Enemy Eaters: Phagocytes & Granulocytes

Phagocytes like monocytes and macrophages kill large enemy cells by engulfing and digesting them. Macrophages are multi-tasking immune cells. Apart from cleansing the body of debris and aged blood cells, they also secrete chemicals to summon other immune cells to the battle site. Granulocytes, such as neutrophils, eosinophils and basophils, destroy invaders with potent chemical granules. For example, pus from an infection contains dead neutrophils and other war debris.

Our immune system continues to baffle scientists due to its ability to mount such an exceptionally coordinated and effective defense against invaders.

Despite the marvels of modern science, there is still no substitute for the immune system. It is extremely critical that we protect our internal army and keep it in prime condition.

Any army needs high morale to win. So does the immune system. Sufficient rest, stress control and positive thinking can help to ensure that our immune system functions properly. Even more important is the quality of fuel and nourishment that our immune army receives on a daily basis. Ask a malnourished soldier to stand up for his country and chances are he will soon collapse. This underlines the importance of a well-balanced, highly nutritious diet. Without it, our body's fighters will not receive sustenance and strength to constantly battle deadly invaders.

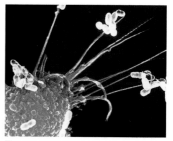

The macrophage is the garbage man of the body

2. How A Battle Is Fought

To better understand the immune system, let us take a simplified look at how it fights a cold virus:

A macrophage grabs and engulfs an invading cold virus using its numerous tentacles. This cleansing role makes the macrophage almost like a garbage man of the body.

Macrophage

Virus

Cell

The macrophage signals other immune cells to the battlefield by displaying pieces of the digested virus (also known as "antigen") on its surface.

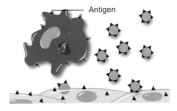

Antigen

A helper T cell responds to this call for help, and binds to the macrophage.

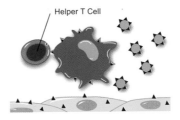

Helper T Cell

Interleukin, tumor necrosis factor and interferon are immune chemicals produced during the helper T cell-macrophage union.

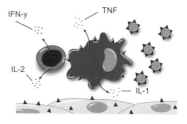

Other immune cells now multiply thanks to the presence of these immune chemicals. During the multiplication of B cells, antibodies are produced.

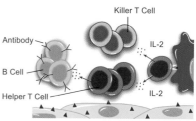

Killer T cells drill holes into virus-infected cells. The virus is now more easily overwhelmed.

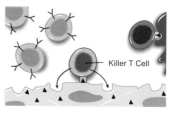

Antibodies (immunoglobulins) lock onto the viruses and signal complements to destroy the viruses and macrophages to engulf them.

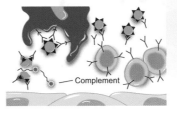

The infection is brought under control. Suppressor T cells turn off activated immune cells. Some B and T cells remain as memory cells, remembering the characteristics of the virus. This information is stored so that the immune system can more quickly respond to and defeat the same virus strain should it attack again. Such a memory mechanism is also employed when vaccines are injected into the body.

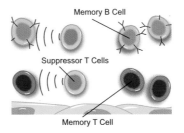

Nutritional Immunology & A Healthy Life

Chapter 3　The Invisible Enemy

Flu is usually accompanied by symptoms like fever, cough, fatigue, muscle ache and even breathlessness. When these symptoms subside in three to five days, we automatically, but incorrectly, assume that the flu is one of life's minor nuisances.

But flu and other viral infections are deadlier than that. In 2001, The World Health Organization (WHO) reported that 10% of adults in the world had at least one incidence of flu and that between 200,000 and 500,000 people die of the flu each year. The Centers for Disease Control and Prevention (CDC) estimates 50,000 American adults will be hospitalized for pneumonia every year. And annually, 200,000 hepatitis A infections are reported in the US alone. Food-borne ailments leading to diarrhea and vomiting affect about 76 million Americans, of which over 5,000 die. The CDC says that flu complications can also lead to other serious illnesses like pneumonia, congestive heart failure and asthma.

Another serious viral infection is SARS, which killed about 900 people within a few months in 2003. SARS usually produces a high fever (at least 38 degrees Celsius or 100.4 degrees Fahrenheit), a dry cough, difficulty breathing, and/or shortness of breath. Early detection helps doctors monitor, treat and ensure that the immune system can defeat the SARS virus. Although several medicines are used in the treatment of SARS, an effective cure has yet to be found.

1. The Incurable Common Cold

The Role Of Cold Medicines

It is usually irritating to have a cold — especially with disturbing symptoms like runny nose, persistent sneezing and overall lethargy. Our first reaction would be to end the suffering with cold medicines, cough suppressants or antibiotics. However, because a virus causes a cold, it cannot be cured by antibiotics as antibiotics only kill bacteria. Cold medicines can suppress symptoms, but they do not kill the virus. In fact, taking cold medicine could potentially prolong your cold! Experts agree that minor colds should not be blindly treated — they will disappear on their own after a few days.

Sneezing, sniffling and the need to clear the throat are actually the body's way of informing us that it is fighting a virus. Such symptoms allow the body to get rid of the viral invader.

Sneezing throws it out of the respiratory tract while mucus of a runny nose and throat phlegm contain many trapped viruses that we easily expel. The pill you take does not stop the cold, it only puts a temporarily stop to the symptoms. By stopping an urge to sneeze, you are preventing your body from expelling the invaders!

Is Fever Medicine Necessary?

Experts define a fever as having a body temperature of 37.7 degrees Celsius (or 99.9 degrees Fahrenheit) or more. Even a mild fever can be uncomfortable, espe- cially when accompanied by body aches, burning eyes or other symptoms. It is tempt- 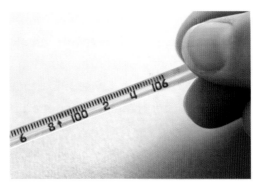 ing to take medication to relieve your fever and bring your temperature down. However, researchers at the Mayo Foundation for Medical Education and Research, the Johns Hopkins Children's Center and the Johns Hopkins Department of Pediatrics advise not to suppress a fever without knowing its cause as this could lead to more harm than good.

A fever is not an illness by itself; it is usually a sign that your immune system is hard at work. Invading agents like cold-causing viruses thrive in cool environments. During an infection, the immune system raises the body's temperature by secreting certain chemicals. This in turn, slows down an invader's ability to reproduce. By producing a low-grade fever, your body may actually be working diligently to eliminate invaders. When you indiscriminately lower a fever, you may help the virus reproduce more rapidly and thus, make it more difficult for your body's immune system to overcome the infection. Furthermore, an elevated body temperature may also increase the production and activity of immune cells. But caution is advised. Extremely high body temperature may also cause damage by denaturing the body's enzymes.

Should A Cough Be Suppressed?

More often than not, a cough is an ordinary immune reflex. Just as sneezing ejects viruses from the nose, coughing ejects them from the lungs and throat. Coughing is also an extremely effective means of clearing irritations or obstructions from our airways. Productive coughs can expel large amounts of phlegm or yellowish pus from our throat, helping us get rid of infectious substances. The US National Institutes of Health advises that productive coughing should not be suppressed by cough medications. Furthermore, indiscriminate use of cough medicine can lead to addiction.

However, experts advise that if a cough lasts for over two weeks or comes from a child, it should be checked by a healthcare professional.

2. Viruses And Bacteria

Flu symptoms may initially appear very much like pneumonia or SARS. However, pneumonia is caused by bacteria while SARS is caused by a virus.

So how do we differentiate a bacterial infection from a viral infection? Is one more dangerous than the other? Though many people lump the two together, in reality, these microscopic invaders are as different as goldfish and elephants.

Structural Difference

Bacteria are much larger than viruses. Most bacteria measure from 0.1 microns to 10 microns (a micron is one millionth of a meter). Viruses usually range from 0.02 microns to 0.2 microns. If you take the average virus to be the size of a human being, the average bacteria would be as large as a 10-story building!

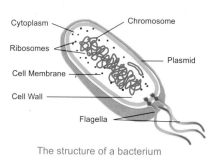

The structure of a bacterium

Bacteria are also more complex organisms than viruses. They are living entities that have all the necessary genetic machinery to reproduce by themselves. They do this by splitting into two cells once every 20 to 30 minutes. In comparison, viruses only have a protein coat and a limited amount of genetic material, which is either DNA or RNA.

Viruses are often classified as non-living and cannot reproduce by themselves; rather, they multiply by invading a host cell and hijacking the host's machinery.

Viruses Could Be Deadlier

Bacteria are mostly harmless to humans. There are countless species of bacteria that live around us. Harmless and helpful bacteria may be found in our

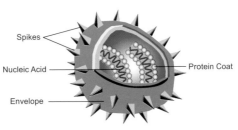

The structure of a common virus

intestines, skin and inside all our major body orifices. They stop other disease-causing bacteria from getting inside us and help us produce much-needed vitamin K. In total, there are only about 30 types of bacteria found to be harmful to humans. Researchers agree that it is viruses that almost always cause new and lethal diseases.

Bacterial and viral infections are usually transmitted through close and direct contact, such as via contaminated hands.

Once on your hands, a bacteria or virus is easily passed to your nose, mouth, eyes or other weakness in the skin's first line of defense. In fact, everyday actions like touching door handles and tabletops can contaminate our hands.

Will Wearing A Facemask Protect Me?

Popular brands of surgical masks are designed to protect against bacteria measuring three microns or more. Viruses are filterable agents, being smaller than 0.2 microns. The N95 facemask used by healthcare workers against the SARS coronavirus in 2003 was designed to protect against particles measuring 0.3 microns or more. Research shows that viruses usually range between 0.02 microns and 0.2 microns, making the effectiveness of the N95 mask questionable.

3. Viruses, Cancer And AIDS

Cancer

Cancer is a disease of genetic mutation. Some viruses cause cancer by mutating the genome of the host cell. About 20% of cancers are linked to viruses and about 80% of these cancers are of the cervix and liver. Examples of viruses leading to cancer include the Epstein-Barr virus (EBV) which is a member of the herpes family and linked to Burkitt's lymphoma tumors; hepatitis B virus linked to hepatocellular carcinoma; human immune deficiency virus (HIV) linked to Kaposi's sarcoma; and human papillomaviruses linked to genital and cervical cancers.

In cancer, part of the mutation involves increased growth and multiplication. Uncontrolled replication of host cells finally leads to the formation of tumors. A tumor is

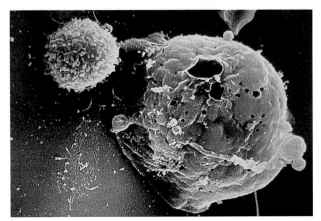

An NK cell (left) and a cancer cell (right)

simply a location whereby a single cancer cell has multiplied and taken over the area. As the tumor grows, it compresses the surrounding non-cancerous tissue. If left untreated, the cancer cells may ultimately take over the entire body. Usually, cancer never gets that far because its growth inhibits the functioning of organs, and the body cannot continue functioning at a certain point when cancer overtakes a vital organ.

Normally there are two kinds of tumors, malignant and benign. Malignant tumors spread via the flow of lymph fluid or blood, and can begin forming another tumor.

Benign tumors are usually less of a threat than malignant ones; they do not reproduce and spread as quickly or as uncontrollably. But benign tumors still pose a threat to patients because they may inhabit, block or compress the tissues of vital organs. Additionally, benign tumors can turn malignant. Due to these dangers, all tumors should be examined and closely monitored. The earlier a tumor is found, the more the treatment options available.

We are fortunate that to a large extent, our body has the ability to locate, neutralize and repair mutated cells, and to fight actual cancer cells. Even with such ability, we may not be able to overcome the challenge of cancer if our immune system is weak.

AIDS (Acquired Immune Deficiency Syndrome)

The virus that leads to AIDS is called the human immunodeficiency virus (HIV). HIV plays its lethal game by slowly and surely causing the immune system to shut down. Once the virus enters and assaults the body's white blood cells, it commands them to replicate into a guerrilla army of new viruses. These viruses wear a camouflage of protein which confuses our own virus-fighting defenses,"antibodies", into thinking that they are harmless.

While viruses can evolve tens of thousands of times faster than plants or animals, few evolve as fast as HIV. When confronted by the immune system, the virus quickly mutates out of the range of the immune system's defensive maneuvers, rendering the body helpless against any form of infection.

41

Just a few years ago, experts universally agreed that AIDS always led to death. But thanks to research, there is hope for AIDS victims. The first indication that the disease could be tamed, if not cured, came when scientists discovered that they could prevent pneumocystis pneumonia—a killer disease common in those with AIDS. Scientists have also achieved some success in preventing other secondary infections in HIV and AIDS patients such as a lung ailment called mycobacterium avium complex.

Unfortunately, lack of nutrition in third world countries is also causing an upsurge in HIV positive and AIDS cases. Experts believe one reason AIDS has such a strong foothold in

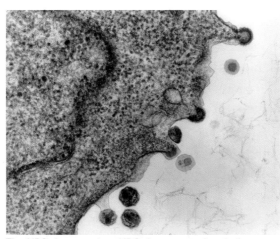

Africa is because protein-calorie malnutrition is widespread there. This form of malnutrition can depress total white blood cell

The AIDS virus — mature AIDS viruses reproduce in the body's lymphoid tissue

count and reduce T cell function, actions that disable the body from attacking a virus.

A properly nourished, healthy immune system is therefore, our only hope in the fierce battle against HIV. With a healthy immune system, the possibility exists that we may be able to rally against this deadly virus.

In the fight against disease, no weapon is more powerful than the human immune system. Absolutely nothing can take its place. When functioning properly, the immune system has all the ammunition it needs to ward off disease, combat illness and overcome the constant attacks of environmental pollutants and toxins. Its sophistry can help us prevent the most dangerous viral invasions and even the potential to get cancer or AIDS. It is up to us to safeguard it well by eating nutritiously and living a healthy and happy life.

Section 2
Strengthening Our Defenses

natural balance

Nutritional Immunology
& A Healthy Life

Chapter 4 Nutritional Immunology

Nothing comes close to a healthy immune system in defending us from disease-causing agents. So how do we keep the immune system in tip-top condition?

A seemingly healthy outward appearance is no indication of how healthy we really are inside. Diseases have a way of sneaking up on us. Infections could be lurking deep within with the only hints being slight tiredness or a persistent sniffle. Before we know it, we could fall seriously ill but by then, it would be too late for prevention. Therefore, we need to stay vigilant by nourishing our immune system daily with generous servings of the right nutrients.

Ever since antibiotics were discovered, humans have been focusing more on treatment and less on prevention. We have forgotten to take advantage of the amazing preventive and healing powers of the immune system. Nutritional Immunology is a relatively new science that emphasizes prevention over cure. This science focuses on the explicit link between proper nutrition and the health of the immune system.

1. Nutrition And The Immune System

Nutrition plays an important role in fighting infections. The absence of any one nutrient will have unfavorable effects on the immune system. However, Nutritional Immunology does not focus on our need for basic nutrients like carbohydrates, proteins, essential fats, vitamins and minerals. A deficiency in these basic nutrients may negatively impact the immune system but in this day and age, most people do not lack these nutrients.

The nutrients we usually miss are disease-fighting nutrients like antioxidants, phytochemicals and polysaccharides. These are the nutrients that, according to Nutritional Immunology, enhance the functions of our immune cells.

How Diet Affects Immunity

Of all the factors contributing to the rise of diseases, inadequate food seems to be the most significant. Wide usage of preservatives, insecticides and highly processed foods affect our ability to digest and absorb essential nutrients. Our immune system desperately needs these nutrients to work efficiently.

Scientists have proven that malnutrition and ingesting pollutants can lead to a vast number of ailments, including autoimmune diseases such as systemic lupus erythometosus, rheumatic fever and glomerulonephritis. In lab animals, a balanced diet is widely used to prevent and treat infection, prevent the development of secondary lesions in autoimmune diseases and fight the growth of tumors.

A healthy immune system responds swiftly and effectively towards infections. But a malnourished immune system will become an easy target for germs. Getting proper nutrition on a regular basis is therefore, absolutely critical. Seeking such nutrients only when we are sick may be too late.

A study on African children showed that malnutrition in the formative years could damage the immune system and lead to recurring respiratory and intestinal infections. Such damage to the immune system is often irreparable.

Many studies prove that this vicious cycle of malnutrition and infection is difficult to break. For example, say experts, although a malnourished baby can be sustained through its mother's milk, when it is eventually given cow's milk or porridge at a later age, the baby's immune system will be weakened. This can lead to more serious infections, hinder the baby's growth, and escalate the baby's risk for diarrhea and diseases.

The Immune Difference

In a war, the stronger party will be victorious. The same applies to our body. It is important to ensure that our immune system can kick into combat mode at any given moment and win the battle. A weak immune system not only increases risk for bacterial or viral infections but also heart disease and cancer. It has

been reported that cancer and heart disease combined kill at least 4,000 Americans a day!

Yearly, one in four Americans die of cancer. Worldwide, in the year 2000, cancer killed seven million people and affected another 10 million. The most common types of cancer are lung cancer, breast cancer, colon cancer, skin cancer, ovarian cancer and prostate cancer.

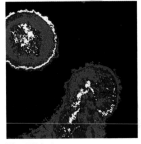

The HIV virus

Research shows that people with cancer can be healthy and cancer-free after a few years despite being told they have only three months to live. Similarly, although some people are HIV positive, they remain AIDS-free even after 10 years. This emphasizes the fact that if the immune system is strong, it can resist many life-threatening illnesses.

2. Modern Challenges To Immunity

Environmental Pollution

Rapid population growth can bring ill effects upon the environment. Experts estimate that the quality of the environment will drop by one percent with every two percent increase in population. Although industrial development increases convenience, it also creates pollution. Industrial waste is often released either into the air, water or soil.

Farming also involves liberal use of insecticides and chemical fertilizers to improve harvests. Large quantities of antibiotics and hormones are used to hasten animal growth. At the same time, forests are being destroyed to increase grain production to feed farm animals. Increase in farm animals, in turn, leads to increase in animal waste that also harms the environment. Currently, there are far more farm animals than humans and farm animals produce about six

times the waste humans do. Nitrates within the waste are harmful when they enter our drinking water. Besides causing disabilities, nitrates also destroy many types of fish as well as other sea creatures.

Stress

Stress can actually be quite good for us. The American Institute of Stress explains that when we are stressed, our pulse rate increases and blood rushes to the brain, improving decision-making capabilities. Blood sugar rises to give us more energy.

As blood is not immediately needed for digestion, it travels rapidly to large arm and leg muscles to provide increased strength, speed and energy. In ancient times, these responses helped humans to deal with sudden attacks, for instance, from predatory animals.

In modern times, stress tends to arise from psychological factors like broken marriages or financial difficulties. Such repeated anxiety causes our normal stress reactions to become harmful, triggering stroke, heart attack, diabetes and ulcers. Chronic stress can impair the immune system's ability to fight diseases. Scientists say stress causes the human body to secrete corticosteroid, a hormone that suppresses immune function and increases risk of getting cancer and influenza.

Unhealthy Diets

The modern diet is filled with fatty food. This could be because people misinterpret nutrition to mean more of meat or milk products. Hence, we absorb more calories than we need. At the same time, we consume too little of fruits and green leafy vegetables and exercise less.

Plant foods are ideal as they contain all of the essential nutrients we need as well as healthy helpings of fiber. A diet rich in animal products will actually cause over absorption of protein, which burdens the kidneys. Animal products are also high in fat, causing increased lipid levels, cardiovascular diseases and weaker immunity.

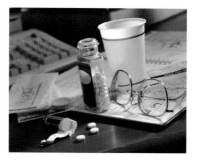

Dependence On Medicines

Unfortunately, when people try to cure diseases caused by unhealthy diets, they usually only succeed in treating the symptoms. For instance, when we are gloomy or suffer from insomnia or fatigue, we might think that popping a pill will help. Although pills sometimes succeed in helping us lose weight, treat an ulcer, or become calmer, they seldom resolve the root cause of our ailment.

Only the immune system knows exactly how, when and where to take appropriate action to resolve illness or fatigue. Unlike the immune system, drugs can only achieve a single purpose, such as stimulating the immune system or suppressing it. Drugs are also very often accompanied by harmful side effects. Sometimes, these side effects are even more dangerous than the conditions that demand treatment.

Vaccines

When bacteria or viruses enter the body, the immune system reacts by producing antibodies to destroy them. Some of our immune cells have a memory response that can last a lifetime. This enables the body to fight future infections caused by the same strain of bacterium or virus.

Vaccinations are based on this theory. Vaccines are usually made using dead or weakened bacteria or viruses to trick our immune system into producing antibodies against them. Common vaccines include the Poliomyelitis Vaccine, Tetanus Vaccine, Chickenpox Vaccine and Influenza Vaccine.

However, rapid mutations of viruses pose a great challenge to vaccine development. This is why doctors advise us to get an annual flu shot — to fight new flu virus strains that could take us by surprise. A vaccine normally offers a good measure of protection against certain diseases and can be quite harmless to the body, with only minor side effects like swelling at the vaccination site or low-grade fever. However, there have been reports of vaccine-related complications. For example, in 1999, Wyeth Laboratories withdrew its vaccine against Rotavirus—a lethal diarrhea-causing virus—after it

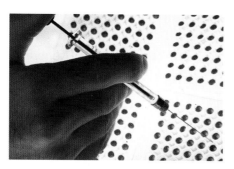

was found that the product could cause fatal intestinal blockage.

Striking A Balance

If health is our goal, then we must rethink the way we live. Medical advancements have brought mankind a false sense of security. Drugs are viewed as a safe substance that can quickly treat illnesses. We sometimes do not realize the harm that can accompany such treatment. Unfortunately, a side-effect-free treatment is a rarity. And once the immune system is damaged, the road to recovery is a long and difficult one.

The key to good health is in our hands. Seeking proper nutrition is an easy and effective step to ensure that we strengthen our defenses in a safe and natural way.

Fortunately, we have a guide in Nutritional Immunology. This science of "self-defense" teaches us how to choose our food wisely. It also emphasizes that there is no better cure for diseases than prevention.

57

Nutritional Immunology
& A Healthy Life

Chapter 5　What Is Proper Nutrition?

Research has long shown that a diet rich in a large variety of plant foods can enhance health without any harmful side effects. This is because plant foods contain an abundance of antioxidants, phytochemicals and polysaccharides; nutrients appointed by Nature to help us prevent diseases.

How we eat will determine how we feel, look and act every day. So, in consuming plant foods, we revitalize our immune system because plant foods aid digestion and flush out toxins. In contrast, consuming too many animal products and high-fat foods will impair immunity, leaving us in a tired, lethargic state.

Though we demand the best quality fuel for our cars, why don't we also pamper our internal engine with the best quality nutrients?

1. Nutritional Do's And Don'ts

Power Up On Fiber

Fiber is a type of carbohydrate found only in plant foods. Fruits (such as apples and bananas), vegetables, psyllium husk, whole grain bread, cereals, legumes (such as kidney beans, chickpeas and lentils) and nuts are particularly rich in fiber.

There are two types of fiber—soluble and insoluble. Soluble fiber, such as pectin, mucilage and algal polysaccharide, absorbs water. Its texture is soft and gluey like that of cooked oat bran or kidney beans. Insoluble fiber, such as cellulose, hemicelluloses and lignin does not absorb water. Psyllium husk, barley, oat, wheat, apple skin and nuts are chewy due

to their content of insoluble fiber. Besides enhancing digestion, insoluble fiber has a restorative effect on the colon and large intestine as it loosens stools and lessens the pressure placed on colon walls.

Fiber content can vary according to a plant's type and growth stage. Usually, the parts that we throw away, such as seeds, the skin

and bran layers of cereals are those with the highest fiber content.

High-fiber foods can help the body regulate blood sugar. Research proves that roughage slows down the absorption of carbohydrates, which then prevents a blood sugar rush. As fiber fills you up quickly, it can curb appetite and aid in weight control. In addition, fiber itself contains zero calories.

Studies link fiber with the prevention of life-threatening diseases like colon cancer as well as breast cancer, diabetes and coronary heart disease. Soluble fiber can reduce the body's level of low-density lipoprotein—a substance that can trigger heart disease. The American Dietetic Association and the US Department of Agriculture suggest that eating as much as 35 grams of fiber a day can greatly reduce the risk of chronic diseases. Unfortunately, a love for fast food and animal products leaves many Americans eating less than 11 grams of fiber daily.

Downside To Animal Products
Protein plays a critical role in the body's physiological processes-such as organism growth and cellular repair.

Protein is generally known to benefit the body. However, nutritionists warn that animal protein can harm the body.

One example is cow's milk. Protein in cow's milk is called casein while protein in human breast milk is called lactalbumin. Nursing infants can digest up to 90% of lactalbumin. But the body is usually only able to digest about 50% of casein. In addition, as commercial cow's milk is heat-treated to kill bacteria, the heat also damages natural enzymes that help us to absorb casein. Undigested casein paves the way for allergic reactions in young children and studies have shown that cow's milk allergy is one of the most common food allergies in kids.

Animal products are also not necessarily the best sources of calcium. Calcium helps us prevent osteoporosis. Many consider cow's milk to be the only source of calcium. But statistics show that osteoporosis flourishes in countries that drink a lot of cow's milk.

From as early as the 19th century, scientists have warned that a diet rich in animal protein will cause calcium to be lost through urine, causing calcium deficiency. Therefore, as cow's milk is high in animal protein, increasing your intake of cow's milk will not necessarily replenish calcium. It can actually increase risk of osteoporosis.

Plant foods are excellent protein and calcium powerhouses. Beans and legumes are very rich in easy-to-digest plant proteins. Soybeans are one example. Weight for weight, soybeans are said to yield twice the protein of meat, four times that of eggs and 12 times that of milk. Soybeans are also low in fat and high in fiber. Soymilk makes a delicious source of calcium. Green vegetables such as broccoli also offer high-quality calcium that is easily absorbed by the body.

High Fat Is Low Nutrition

The mass media constantly reminds us to eat at least 5 servings of fruits and vegetables a day. Unfortunately, about 80 percent of Americans do not heed this advice. And they are not the only ones that don't.

The World Health Organization (WHO) and the United Nations Food and Agriculture Organization

63

(FAO) are worried that rapid urbanization in developing countries is causing traditionally vegetarian and low-fat diets to change to meat-rich, high-fat ones. High-fat diets are closely associated with obesity, heart disease and some cancers. The primary risk factor for heart disease is a diet high in saturated fat and cholesterol.

According to a 2003 WHO-FAO report, China and India are among countries with a plant food intake of less than 400g a day. At the same time, the rate of heart disease in China and India is higher than that in all developed countries put together. India is also believed to have the highest number of diabetics in the world. In utter contrast, South Korea enjoys a relatively low rate of chronic diseases compared to countries of equal economic status as Koreans continue to eat a diet rich in plant foods.

The WHO-FAO report also suggests that food high in fat and salt will increase risk of type 2 diabetes while high-fiber food and green leafy vegetables lower this risk. The report proposes eating more plant foods to reduce risk of cancer. The Annals of Internal Medicine adds that eating an extra serving of fruits or vegetables a day cuts the risk for heart disease by four percent. Furthermore, plant foods also help type 2 diabetics to prevent heart disease.

Natural Isn't Always Safe

The most effective way to achieve proper nutrition is to eat wholesome and natural plant foods. Plant foods are most suitable because they can equip us with nutrients in a natural way unlike chemically extracted vitamins or tonics.

There are however, many misconceptions about plants. Although plants are natural, not all of them are safe or healthy enough to be consumed as a plant food. For example, tobacco leaves, coca leaf (the source of cocaine), hemp (the source of marijuana) and opium poppy (the source of heroin and morphine) are unsafe natural ingredients.

Plants are, therefore, available in two varieties: plant foods or food herbs that do not give harmful side effects and medicinal plants or herbs, which can bring harm when formulated or used incorrectly. Below are some examples of plants to avoid:

Caffeine-Rich Plants

Tea is a very popular beverage worldwide. But Camellia leaf, the ingredient most widely used in many types of commercial teas, contains three-and-a-half percent caffeine by weight — that is about one percent more caffeine than popular coffee

beans. From a Nutritional Immunology perspective, this makes tea leaves natural but unsafe.

Caffeine is consumed as a "pick-me-up" because of its stimulating effects on the nervous system. But caffeine can cause undesirable side effects like anxiety, insomnia, irregular heartbeat, addictiveness and even death in those with high blood pressure. There are strong signs that caffeine raises cholesterol and leads to heart disease. As caffeine affects the liver and pancreatic function, it can lead to blood sugar imbalance and as a result, chronic fatigue. As yet, there is no direct link between caffeine and cancer. But caffeine can obstruct DNA repair—a process that can lead to cancer.

Ephedra

Ephedra is also known by its Chinese name, Ma Huang. It contains the active ingredient ephedrine, which is found in some diet pills. By claiming that ephedrine "enhances energy" and "burns calories the natural way", weight loss pill makers mask the potentially deadly effects of this herb.

Clinical studies show that ephedra can cause heart attack, blood toxicity and bleeding stroke. The FDA has also collected over 150 ephedra-linked death reports. Neurology, the official publication of the American Academy of Neurology, says that just 32 milligrams of ephedra per day can increase stroke risk. Nevertheless, ephedra pill labels suggest taking up to 100 milligrams a day. The US federal government has now banned the use of ephedra as a dietary supplement.

Guar Gum

Guar gum is a weight-loss ingredient that was banned in the 1990s. Guar gum is a complex sugar that swells when wet, creating a feeling of fullness when eaten. However, its side effects include frightening instances of stomach, throat and intestinal blockage.

Exercise is the best way to lose weight

White Willow Bark

White willow bark contains salicylic acid, the active ingredient in aspirin. The FDA says that this herb is sometimes used in child medications that are labeled aspirin-free. White willow bark can induce internal bleeding in aspirin-sensitive adults. The National Council Against Health Fraud cautions that using white willow bark for childhood chicken pox or influenza can lead to Reye's syndrome, a disease which affects all organs of the body, but most lethally the liver and the brain.

Variety And Purity

Although plants contain many nutrients required by the immune system, there is no particular plant that can accommodate all of our nutritional needs. Therefore, scientists say that we must consume at least 10 to 15 different types of plant foods daily for an adequate supply of nutrients.

For those who don't eat enough plant foods, we feel that we must supplement our diet with refined foods and/or multivitamins. However, this is not only inadequate but also, potentially harmful to the body:

Limitations Of Refined Foods

Although food processing prolongs the shelf life of a food, it destroys key nutrients. When nutrients are removed from their sources, they become chemicals and could disappear to varying extents. Added nutrients in refined foods only imitate those found in plant foods. In the long run, nutrient extracts cannot play substitute to the nutrition provided by wholesome food.

When we eat a combination of wholesome plant foods, we are also consuming a combination of different antioxidants, phytochemicals and polysaccharides. In the same vein, when we consume different species of the same plant, we may be obtaining different benefits. For example, there are many varieties of ginseng. Korean ginseng warms the body while

Siberian ginseng is cooling. Ji-Lin ginseng has a combination of both hot and cold properties.

This is why Nutritional Immunology stresses that we should eat different types of plant foods to enhance health.

The selection, preparation and formulation of different plants require a certain degree of professional knowledge. How we formulate plants is important since good plant combinations can increase the potential of each ingredient while bad combinations have the reverse effect. Similarly, in product selection, it is necessary to choose products that contain many different plant ingredients to achieve balanced nutrition.

Multivitamins And Extracted Nutrients

Our body can produce some of the vitamins that we need but these are by no means enough for daily bodily functions. Vitamins and other nutrients must therefore, be obtained from a balanced diet. Plant foods can provide us with all the nutrients we need.

However, it has become commonplace to pop a multivitamin pill to either supplement our diet or "make-up" for the nutrients we feel we lack. For example, when we catch a cold, we think that taking a vitamin C pill or vitamin C-enriched orange juice can increase our resistance. However, there is no concrete proof to say that vitamin C cures or prevents the common cold. Experts believe that at the most, vitamin C may only shorten the duration of the cold by half a day.

Experts also caution against purchasing antioxidants in pill form. Evidence shows that antioxidant pills cannot provide all the nutrients found in wholesome plants and in addition, can cause toxic side effects. For example, beta-carotene, which occurs naturally in certain foods like carrots, is said to prevent cancer. But in 1994, the New England Journal of Medicine reported a study in Finland where beta-carotene pills gave male smokers 18% more risk of getting lung cancer. A second study published two years later in the Journal of the National Cancer Institute showed smokers taking both beta-carotene and vitamin A pills to have 28% more risk of lung cancer and 17% increased risk of death compared to those not taking any of the twopills.

The Wholesome Difference

In the Finnish study, later research showed that isolated beta-carotene promotes the activation of carcinogens (substances that cause cancer) in tobacco smoke. This damages DNA. DNA damage is a key step in the mutation of a normal cell to a cancer cell.

Extraction of a nutrient from its original source transforms that nutrient's biochemical structure. Scientists propose that some extracted nutrients, like vitamin C, will oxidize and release billions of free radicals that are harmful to the body. Whereas, when we eat an orange, we obtain vitamin C that is beneficial to the body.

The best nutrients therefore, are those obtained from wholesome foods. Wholesome nutrients are also more easily absorbed. In the case of an orange, it contains not just vitamin C but a host of powerful phytochemicals liked-limonene. It is this natural combination of nutrients that is beneficial to the health of the immune system.

Similarly, the ability of soybean to protect us against diseases stems not just from one phytochemical but many, and even today, scientists still have no idea how many. When a single phytochemical is extracted, it may lead to the destruction of other nutrients.

71

To be truly good for us, vitamins must exist in synergy with other nutrients like antioxidants, phytochemicals and polysaccharides - therefore, too much or too little of one nutrient will cause nutritional imbalance in the body.

Studies show that we absorb natural vitamin-nutrient bonds better than synthetic vitamin pills. Dr. Abram Hoffer, an expert in orthomolecular medicine, says that, "Components of food do not exist freely in nature; nature does not lay down pure protein, pure fat or pure carbohydrates. Their molecules are interlaced in a very complex three-dimensional structure. Intermingled are the essential nutrients such as vitamins and minerals, again not free, but combined in complex molecules."

The goal of Nutritional Immunology is to promote the consumption of natural and safe plant foods that are rich in antioxidants, phytochemicals and polysaccharides. These nutrients should not be chemically processed to ensure that they are easily and safely absorbed by the human body.

2. How Plant Foods Are Selected

While guiding scientists on the selection processes of plant foods, Nutritional Immunology also advocates the best harvesting and processing procedures to retain the optimum quality and quantity of antioxidants, phytochemicals and polysaccharides.

Growth And Harvest

Every plant has an ideal growing environment and time. Harvesting affects nutrient quality, thus, plants should ideally be harvested when nutrients are most plentiful.

Rice and barley as well as mushrooms like Reishi contain the most nutrients when they are tender. In contrast, ginseng must be grown for at least six years before its root has any nutritional value. Similarly, an Opuntia cactus fruit needs a minimum of four years to develop and ripen before its nutrients can be tapped. Fruits like bananas are most nutritious when they ripen on trees as compared to picking them when they are green.

Even the harvesting hour can be critical — for instance, cactus pads are usually harvested earlier in the day to minimize acidity.

73

Some farmers attempt to speed up plant growth with stimulants and fertilizers. This may shorten the plant's growth period but it will greatly reduce its nutritional value.

Plant Species

More than just identifying a nutritious herb, Nutritional Immunology experts focus on the species that is particularly nutritious. For example, there are over 80 species of ginger and at least 1,000 varieties of mulberry. Although similar in characteristics, different species will contain different sets of nutrients. With some plants, only a few species are edible or outstanding in terms of nutritional value.

For example, of the various types of ginseng, Panax Ginseng and Panax Quinquefolius are said to be the most nutritious.

Or for instance, within the same Opuntia cactus family, there are some whose fruits are edible and others, like Opuntia Compressa, whose fruits cannot be eaten. Comprehensive knowledge is also needed when using mushrooms — Coriolus Versicolor and Agaricus Blazel Murill are extremely beneficial to health while Amanita mushrooms can kill when eaten.

The Best Parts

Some of the most nutritious parts of plants are the leaf of the mulberry tree, the grape seed, cactus juice and the fruit of the ginseng. OPC, an antioxidant found in grape seeds, is effective against heart and retinal diseases. The pads of Opuntia cacti have a different nutrient composition as compared to the fruits.

For many years, the ginseng root was considered the most valuable. But recent research has shown the ginseng berry to be better — the berry contains four times more immunity supporting ginsenosides than the root. Ginseng berry is also said to promote digestion and blood circulation and normalize blood sugar.

Experts also recommend keeping the skins of fruits and vegetables, as they are very nutritious. However, they must be washed with a high-quality vegetable cleanser to remove the remains of fertilizers and insecticides.

We can make better-informed decisions about nutrition by understanding the manufacturing process of plant foods and the plant parts we consume. Experts feel that nutrients such as dietary fiber, vitamin B and phytochemicals present in wheat husk will be lost during the milling process. Even if fiber and vitamins are added later, they cannot replace the nutrients found in the husks.

Plant Processing

Processing can affect nutrient content. For some plants, soaking in water for too long destroys nutrients; for others, heat degrades nutritional value.

Concentrating nutrients can also

increase or decrease nutritional quality. A 10-year-old ginseng that has been concentrated two times is still more nutritious than a three-year-old ginseng that has been concentrated 10 times. A plant that has been boiled for a long time will not be high in either nutrients or viscosity. At the same time, if the wrong plant part is used, high concentration will not provide higher nutritional value.

Storage

Plants are naturally difficult to store. Nutrients may diminish if plants are not stored in a dark, cool and dry place before processing. Even then, in some instances, such as for corn, nutritional value will drop after three days of storage. When supermarkets attempt to prolong the shelf life of vegetables, they keep them in a moist condition, which can destroy nutrients. It is therefore, important to know how much moisture is needed to keep vegetables adequately fresh.

Researchers have found that when plants are not imme-diately consumed, freezing is the best storage option. Freeze drying preserves nutrients that are destroyed by heat. Water exists in three states: ice, liquid and vapor. Freeze drying allows the frozen water content of plant foods to turn into vapor directly from its solid state. This way, the original aroma, color and shape of the plants are retained. However, this method cannot be used on soybeans. Beans contain a toxin that can only be destroyed by heating them to 60 degrees Celsius or more. A process called spray drying is more suitable for plants that need heat to destroy toxins. Spray drying involves transforming a substance from liquid to powder through continuous blending and drying.

Heating

Some plants use toxins as a way of self-preservation. These toxins are usually destroyed through cooking. Some plants must be cooked while others cannot. For example, boiling cactus will lead to nutrient loss but ginseng will remain nutritious even after heating.

Overheating food generally destroys the chemical structure of some nutrients. This is why experts recommend that water used to cook vegetables should not be thrown away as the water may contain more nutrients than the vegetables themselves. In contrast to prolonged cooking, plant foods can retain their nutritional value when stir-fried.

Manufacturers of health food products must be responsible when heating plants. For convenience, they may cook all of their plant ingredients together, using the same temperature. Although this method is suitable for green beans, carrots and lima beans, it will destroy the nutrients of plants that require different cooking temperatures and cooking periods. Therefore, in the pursuit of high quality, well-balanced plant formulations, we should only purchase those that are cooked separately.

The Knowledge Factor

There is a difference between good plant food products and excellent ones. It is easy to manufacture nutritious foods. But it is extremely challenging to select the best plant foods and deliver them to consumers in the purest, freshest, most nutritious form.

Knowledge is critical for the latter. Nature requires our respect and understanding. Only by being careful and aware can we expect to obtain an herb's full nutritional power.

Thanks to Nutritional Immunology, we are beginning to understand what proper nutrition is and how we can prolong the length and quality of our lives through plant foods.

Section 3

Strategies For Nutrition

Nutritional Immunology
& A Healthy Life

Chapter 6 Eating For Balance

All of us know that a balanced diet strengthens the immune system. But how many of us actually put this theory to practice? We tend to forget to obtain adequate nutrients due to our harried lifestyles and eating habits.

It is also common to overeat. It is not how much you eat, but how well you eat that matters. Good health may be easily obtained by following this time-tested rule: choose a low-calorie, high-nutrient, high-fiber diet.

The following strategies can help anyone jump-start healthy eating habits.

1. Obtaining Nutrients

Morning Must Haves

It is important to start the day right by eating a nutritionally-balanced breakfast.

Researchers at the Harvard Medical School discovered that people who took daily breakfast were a third less likely to become obese than those who skipped this meal. This is because eating first thing in the morning is believed to help regulate appetite and enhance energy. Breakfast eaters are also less likely to be hungry throughout the day and hence, less likely to overeat.

Ginseng berry

Having breakfast is also believed to keep blood sugar in check — this prevents diabetes or high cholesterol, which in turn, prevents heart disease. The best benefits, say the researchers, comes from eating whole-grain cereals for breakfast. Whole-grain cereals are rich in fiber, which stabilizes blood sugar, curbs appetite and keeps the heart healthy.

However, it is still important to not overeat for breakfast as this burdens the digestive system and stops it from working optimally.

Nutritional Immunology urges that a healthy breakfast should be highly nutritious without burdening the immune and digestive systems. Nutrients such as phytochemicals and fiber are ideal. Eating ingredients such as ginseng berry, soy and psyllium husk in the morning supplies the body with an ideal amount of phytochemicals and fiber.

Main Meal Wisdom

Having a fiber-rich snack half an hour before lunch or dinner can also stop us from overeating. Apart from ginseng berry, soy and psyllium husk, our meal choices can include more phytochemical-rich cactus, polysaccharide-rich mushrooms as well as antioxidant-rich broccoli, asparagus and leafy vegetables.

If you need to consume meat, choose fish instead of red meat. Studies have linked high consumption of red meat with cancers such as breast and colorectal cancer as well as heart disease. For example, red meat consumption has been said to give Singaporeans 2.2 times more risk of getting colorectal cancer. This is mainly because red meat is very high in saturated fats. Fish, in contrast, contains more heart-healthy fat such as omega-3 fatty acids.

Many think that vegetarians rarely suffer from chronic diseases but this is not true. First, many vegetarians tend to choose the same types of fruits or vegetables without giving themselves a more varied plant food diet. Second, many prepackaged vegetarian foods tend to be over-processed, where valuable nutrients are destroyed. A vegetarian diet also tends to be rich in carbohydrates without sufficient phytochemicals, antioxidants and polysaccharides. It is therefore critical for a vegetarian to choose a diet rich in these disease-fighting nutrients. Supplementing a vegetarian diet with soy also provides phytochemicals and plant protein.

Food Preparation

The way your meal is cooked is also important. Choose foods with less salt and sugar and oil. The American Heart Association cautions that too much salt can lead to high blood pressure, which in turn, can cause stroke and heart disease. We should try to limit our daily total intake of salt to about one-and-a-half teaspoons.

Too much sugar can lead to diabetes and obesity. If you must eat something sweet, be savvy about the type of sugar you are taking. Sugar is a type of carbohydrate. Its most popular varieties are sucrose (such as in sugar cane), glucose (found mainly in grapes) and fructose (found in most fruits and vegetables). All give about 16 calories a teaspoon but fructose has the lowest glycemic index of about 23 compared to sucrose's 67 and glucose's 100. The glycemic index measures how much blood sugar rises after we have eaten a specific food. High-glycemic foods can cause blood sugar spikes, which can lead to diabetes.

Experts always recommend preparing food with as little oil as possible. As such, cooking methods such as steaming, baking, grilling, boiling or stir-frying are advised. If using cooking oil, studies have shown monounsaturated oils like olive or canola and polyunsaturated oils like soy, corn and grape seed to be most beneficial to health. These oils emit less smoke when heated.

2. Convenience vs. Nutrition

In today's fast-paced world, eating in a hurry has become a norm. Apart from what we eat, it is also important to watch how we eat.

The American Dietary Association advises chewing slowly to control food intake. This is because it takes the brain about 20 minutes to realize that we are eating. Once it gets this message, we stop feeling hungry. When we choose smaller meals and chew them slowly, we also give the digestive system sufficient time to secrete relevant enzymes needed for proper digestion. Taking our time when eating will thus help us to curb indigestion, overeating and obesity.

Poor eating habits are a key barrier to nutrient absorption. Many working adults opt for hasty meals taken at a cafeteria near their homes or offices. Some may just grab a sandwich from a convenience store. These are convenience meals designed to keep us from feeling hungry. They are different from nutritious foods designed to keep us healthy. However, despite realizing this, many of us still reach for the foods we usually eat. If we can observe our eating habits and note down areas to be improved, such as choosing an apple instead of a candy bar, we can drastically prevent disorders that arise from poor eating habits.

Let us examine some common dietary mistakes and consider ways to overcome them:

A Balanced Breakfast

A ham and egg sandwich or a meat burger may sound like good choices for breakfast but actually, they are high in fat, and most likely, in salt. Such a breakfast also lacks fiber. If you persist in eating similar high-fat breakfasts, you could be putting yourself at risk of getting heart disease. Introduce some antioxidants and phytochemicals as well

as fiber by including cucumber and tomato slices as well as lettuce in your sandwich and have a fruit with the meal.

Many choose to drink milk for breakfast. Most commercially available milk brands are pasteurized to kill bacteria but this process also destroys natural enzymes that promote nutrient absorption. Pasteurization may also stop the body from absorbing minerals like calcium. Cow's milk is also very high in animal protein that can cause calcium loss through urine. Loss of calcium can lead to the dreaded bone disease, osteoporosis. Drinking soy milk instead of cow's milk supplies the body with

plant protein and lots of immune system-strengthening phytochemicals. Soy milk is also lower in fat.

Chinese breakfasts are known to be leaner but nowadays, food sellers tend to make these meals rich to improve taste. There are many hidden dangers within Chinese breakfasts, such as deep fried dough, porridge or egg-based noodle dishes. Deep-frying uses a lot of fat which is bad for the heart while the healthy-looking porridge may actually be high in salt. Egg-based noodle dishes contain about 1,010 calories per plate, which is almost two-thirds of the daily calorie limit of an adult female.

Power Lunches

Packed lunches are popular options for working adults. These meals can be healthy provided we pack them wisely. Include a small portion of rice that is accompanied by steamed or boiled vegetables. End the meal with a fruit.

Buffets are usually much-anticipated meals. But buffet menus tend to stay the same, depriving us of nutritional variety. Furthermore, a buffet menu would rarely include food that is cooked without oil, sugar or salt. Buffet meals also tend to be very high in cholesterol.

Another popular lunch option is fast food, which today, is available in more affordably priced meal combinations. Having a hamburger, fries and a soft drink can easily add up to over 1,000 calories. When taken regularly, such food not only deprives the immune system of nutrients but can also clog the arteries, cause heart disease and other chronic diseases like obesity, cancer and arthritis. Opting for a salad on a fast food menu is not necessarily healthier. Studies show that such salads can contain even 700 calories — more calories than a hamburger — when smothered with dressing.

These meals may be satisfying but chances are, they will leave you feeling sluggish for the rest of the day. In contrast, a lunch rich in plant foods will energize you, helping you to be more productive at work and at home.

Some people like to have a tea break that sometimes leaves them too full to have a proper dinner. If you feel hungry after lunch and before dinner, try to avoid eating a high-fat, high-sugar snack or beverage. Instead keep some fruits handy for a low-calorie, nutrient-packed, revitalizing snack. Fruits give you a sense  of fullness, and they also digest quickly, allowing you to still have a well-balanced dinner.

Light Nights

Some people consider dinner to be a time to celebrate after a hard day's work. So, they may think nothing about rewarding themselves with a large meal. However, dinner should be eaten wisely to avoid overburdening the digestive system and having difficulty sleeping. To avoid overeating during dinner, it is a very good idea to have a low-calorie, fiber drink just before leaving the office.

If you are having a barbecue or fondue-type of dinner, be wary of hidden salt and fat in sauces and soup bases. Some soup bases contain purine, an ingredient that can affect metabolism.

It is also not a good idea to regularly eat a late night meal as this could burden the digestive system. Our gastric mucosa regenerates once every two or three days. A habit of eating a late night snack can affect the secretion of gastric juices, leading to stomach disorders like gastric ulcers.

If hunger pangs just cannot be ignored, then opt for a light, fiber-rich snack with cereals since these foods will not burden the digestive system.

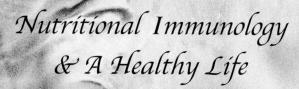

Nutritional Immunology
& A Healthy Life

Chapter 7 Antioxidants, Phytochemicals And Polysaccharides

Our body needs wholesome nutrients to perform perfectly. Apart from strengthening our defenses, these nutrients aid the body in growth and development, cell repair, and a variety of physiological functions.

Many of us think that protein, carbohydrates, vitamins, minerals and fats are the only nutrients we need. Actually, there are three other types of nutrients that our body sorely needs to become an insurmountable fortress against diseases. These nutrients are antioxidants, phytochemicals and polysaccharides.

Why are these nutrients so important to us and how do we obtain them on a safe and regular basis?

1. Antioxidants — Your Fountain Of Youth

What Are Antioxidants?

Antioxidants are compounds that prevent cell damage through oxidation. These compounds neutralize free radicals. Free radicals are highly reactive and unstable molecules produced by cigarette smoke, toxic chemicals, excess sunlight and even our body's own metabolic processes. These molecules can cause the mutation of proteins, membranes and even our own DNA, leading to cancer and other degenerative diseases like cataracts and heart disease. Antioxidants obtained from natural plant sources have been proven to seek out and "anti-oxidize" free radicals to prevent their destructive effect on the body.

The human body manufactures its own set of antioxidants. These antioxidants are called endogenous antioxidants. Endogenous antioxidants are tasked with converting free radicals into harmless oxygen particles and water. Thereafter, endogenous antioxidants will change into less active free particles and leave the body. But for endogenous antioxidants to be fully effective, they must work in synergy with our immune cells to defend and repair free radical damage.

As endogenous antioxidants cannot totally expel excess free radicals, experts advise us to reinforce them with a diet rich in antioxidants. Antioxidants obtained through the diet or external sources are called exogenous antioxidants.

The effect of antioxidants has been likened to that of a vacuum cleaner. For example, studies have shown antioxidants to fight heart disease by stopping cholesterol deposits on blood vessel walls and by lowering overall cholesterol levels. By neutralizing cell-mutating free radicals, antioxidants offer hope in the prevention of cancer.

A diet rich in antioxidants is also said to delay aging. Antioxidants have even been used as anti-inflammatory agents to reduce the severity of arthritis and bronchitis.

Antioxidant Pills vs. Natural Antioxidants

For those who think that popping an antioxidant pill is beneficial, here's news that may make you sit up. Thus far, there is no conclusive evidence to say that antioxidants in pill form can help prevent cancer or other diseases.

For years, scientists have closely compared the use of antioxidants through supplements with that through the diet only to find that antioxidant pills could actually escalate risk of cancer. For example, in 1994, The New England Journal of Medicine reported that artificial beta-carotene supplements actually increased occurrence of lung cancer among heavy smokers in Finland. Therefore, to lower risk of cancer, scientists advise obtaining antioxidants from natural sources such as wholesome plant foods.

Antioxidant Powerhouses

The vitamins C and E, and beta-carotene are some well-known antioxidants. But studies have shown other antioxidants to be more potent.

Oligomeric Proanthocyanidin, better known as OPC, is a powerful antioxidant found in pine bark and grape seeds. In fact, OPC is touted to have 20 times more antioxidant activity than vitamin C and 50 times more antioxidant activity than vitamin E.

Rose, which is actually an edible flower, is also very rich in antioxidants. Rose hips, the small, cherry-like fruit of roses,

are said to have 50 times the amount of vitamin C found in lemons. This high concentration of vitamin C enhances the body's ability to produce collagen, a substance that promotes healthy skin.

Ginseng berry and cactus fruit are two other rich sources of antioxidants. Recent studies have found ginseng berry to have 1.4 times more antioxidant activity than vitamin C and cactus fruit to have seven times more antioxidant activity than vitamin C.

Ginseng berry

Lately, research has shown lycopene, a type of beta-carotene found in tomatoes, to have promising effects in fighting cancer.

2. Phytochemicals — Power From Plants

What Are Phytochemicals?

Phytochemicals, or plant chemicals, are compounds unique to each fruit, vegetable and herb. Antioxidants and phytochemicals give fruits and vegetables their color, flavor and aroma. Phytochemicals protect these plants from sunlight and also ensure their survival. Research has shown phytochemicals to possess enormous healing and disease-preventing properties because of their amazing ability to nourish and bolster the immune system.

There are millions of phytochemicals and science has not even begun to name all of them. However, scientists have grouped the most common phytochemicals into four broad categories, namely indoles, isothiocyanates, flavonoids and isoflavones.

Each plant also contains its own unique variety of phytochemicals. For example, indoles, one of the larger groups of phytochemicals, is available in vegetables such as cauliflower, broccoli, cabbage, and turnips. Indoles-3-carbinol has been known to reduce risk of cancer, such as breast and ovarian cancer, by acting on a precursor to the female hormone estrogen and causing it to break down into a harmless form.

Isothiocyanates comprise two groups: PEITC and sulforaphane. PEITC is found mainly in turnips and cabbage and is shown to inhibit lung cancer and prevent carcinogens from binding to DNA. Sulforaphane, contained in broccoli, cauliflower and cabbage, eliminates carcinogens in cells.

Besides onions and sweet potatoes, flavonoids are also found in citrus fruits and many types of berries. Flavonoids have anti-cancer properties—they prevent cancer-causing hormones from attaching to normal cells. They also inhibit enzymes responsible for cancer cell metastasis.

Isoflavones are found in soybeans. Soy isoflavones like genistein, daidzein and glycitein offer great disease resistance. Other than lowering serum cholesterol levels, they also reduce the probability of coronary heart disease as well as the risk of osteoporosis in postmenopausal women. The American National Cancer Institute is considering using genistein as a cancer-fighting medicine.

While some plants are rich sources of a particular phytochemical, others contain myriads of phytochemicals. For example, a tomato-rich diet has been said to reduce DNA breakdown through oxidation by up to 40%. This is because tomatoes are bestowed with lycopene, a cancer-fighting phytochemical. The prickly pear cactus, in contrast, contains not one beneficial phytochemical but thousands.

It cannot be repeated enough that a varied diet is very important for us to obtain as many varieties of phytochemicals as possible.

Phytochemicals As Cancer Fighters

There are three stages in the formation of a malignant tumor. First, our DNA is damaged and we begin to feel ill. Next, injured cells mutate or grow abnormally. Third, these cells turn into cancerous tumors and spread to other organs.

According to John Potter, an epidemiologist at the University of Minnesota, almost every step on the path to cancer can be retarded or reversed by one or more compounds in fruits or vegetables. Dr Paul Talalay of Johns Hopkins Medical Institution adds, "Now we have wonderful evidence that if you eat more fruits and vegetables, you will have lower risk of cancer in several organ systems."

For instance, indoles found in cruciferous vegetables such as cauliflower and cabbage, have been found to help the body metabolize estrogen to a form that does not trigger breast cancer. In a 1991 study, 12 volunteers who took vegetable extracts containing indoles every day for a week had 50% more of "good" estrogen in their blood.

Phytoestrogens

Some phytochemicals are often referred to as plant hormones.

Many plant hormones work like the human hormone estrogen. Hence, these plant hormones are called phytoestrogens. As women usually experience declining levels of estrogen at about 35 years of age, a phytoestrogen-rich diet can help replenish hormone supply.

Phytoestrogens are also a safer alternative to chemically created hormones. Until 2001, hormone replacement therapy (HRT) was thought to be a boon for postmenopausal women to ease moodiness, hot flashes and keep their bones healthy. Then, a US National Institutes of Health Women's Health Initiative report in July 2002 revealed that HRT use could increase risk of getting heart disease by up to 80% in the first year. Overall, HRT increased risk of breast cancer by 26%, stroke by 41% and heart attack by 29%.

Also, while human estrogen stimulates healthy cell growth, it also stimulates tumor growth when cancer invades the body. As the structure of phytoestrogens is similar to that of human estrogens but less potent, phytoestrogens encourage healthy cell growth while inhibiting tumor growth. By binding to cells where human estrogen typically binds, phytoestrogens mimic the positive roles of human estrogen without the harmful side effects. Phytoestrogens become important as the body secretes less estrogen with age. When women reach their fifties, phytoestrogens may become their main source of hormones.

Apart from preventing cancer, phytoestrogens can also help by firming the skin, stabilizing blood pressure and keeping cholesterol levels healthy. By reducing LDL or "bad" cholesterol, phytoestrogens can lower risk of heart disease. Similarly, phytoestrogens help to retain calcium in the bones and aid calcium absorption, preventing osteoporosis.

3. Polysaccharides — Nature's Antidotes

What Are Polysaccharides?

Polysaccharides are long chains of sugars commonly found in some mushrooms. Research has shown that mushroom polysaccharides can inhibit tumor growth by activating immune cells. Polysaccharides help to balance the immune system and enable it to destroy existing cancer cells and viruses. Polysaccharide-rich mushroom extracts are also used in anti-viral medication.

In the 1960s, scientists discovered that polysaccharides possess anti-cancer properties. However, each type of polysaccharide has its own unique ability and healing effect on certain cancers. Furthermore, the amount of polysaccharides used is important, as only a suitable amount will produce optimal effects.

Among polysaccharide-rich mushrooms, the following five are most lauded for their anti-cancer and anti-viral properties:

Agaricus Blazel Murill (ABM) Mushroom

Researchers at the King Drew Medical Centre, University of California Los Angeles, found that polysaccharides in Agaricus Blazel Murill (ABM) mushrooms help to increase immune cell activity in the body. ABM mushroom, also known as "sun mushroom" and "princess mushroom", is rich in two polysaccharide compounds, beta-1,3 D-glucan and beta-1,6 D-glucan. These polysaccharides restore and support the body's immune system by stimulating the production of virus and cancer-fighting lymphocyte T-cells, helper T-cells, interferon and interleukin.

In a joint study by Tokyo University, National Cancer Center Laboratory and Tokyo College of Pharmacy, lab animals with cancerous tumors were fed ABM mushrooms. The cancerous tumors were eliminated in 90% of the animals. What was more amazing is that when animals were fed ABM mushrooms as a

preventive agent, and then injected with powerful cancer-causing cells, 99.4% of the animals showed no tumor growth because the cancer cells could not even be successfully embedded.

Coriolus Versicolor Mushroom

Coriolus Versicolor mushroom is also called "Yun Zhi mushroom". In the 1970s, researchers isolated a high molecular weight polysaccharide from Coriolus Versicolor's cultured mycelium (the  thread-like extensions). This polysaccharide K (PSK), also known as Krestin, contains a beta-glucan with the main chain consisting of beta (1-4) glucose polymer branched at the positions three and six of the glucose. PSK has been shown to have anti-microbial, anti-viral and anti-tumor properties. It is one of the safest and most effective agents for treating chronic illnesses.

Many studies have shown PSK therapy to inhibit tumor growth when administered prior to tumor implantation. PSK also restored depressed cell mediated immune response in lab animals with tumors and when administered in combination with chemotherapy, PSK made chemotherapy more fruitful. PSK therapy was particularly effective when taken orally.

Shiitake Mushroom

Shiitake mushroom is often called the "nice-smelling mushroom" or "black mushroom". Shiitake mushroom has been used for centuries in Oriental folk medicine to treat colds, flu, poor blood circulation, upset stomach and fatigue.

The mushroom polysaccharide, Lentinan has many immunopotentiating properties including the enhancement of natural killer cells and increased production of gamma interferon.

Researchers claim that Lentinan may recharge the immune system when it has been weakened by chronic illnesses such as chronic fatigue syndrome, long periods of stress, medical treatments involving radiotherapy and chemotherapy or even aging. Research indicates that Lentinan treatment prior to radiation treatment offers protection from reduced white blood cell counts. In the 1980s, the Pharmaceutical Council of Japan approved the use of Lentinan as an anti-cancer drug.

Maitake Mushroom

Maitake mushroom is high in beneficial polysaccharides, beta-glucan as well as other polysaccharides including phospholipids, nucleotides and unsaturated  fatty acids. It can enhance immune function as well as inhibit tumor growth.

Many studies have shown the D-fraction part of the Maitake polysaccharide to work in conjunction with chemotherapy for cancer. In one experiment, the chemotherapy agent, mitomycin was used. Using only D-fraction inhibited tumor growth more effectively by 45% to 80% than using only mitomycin. Combining Maitake with mitomycin enhanced tumor inhibition by almost 98%.

Maitake mushroom is reported to be useful in the treatment or prevention of cancer, AIDS, high blood pressure, diabetes, obesity and high cholesterol.

Ganoderma Lucidum Mushroom

Ganoderma Lucidum mushroom or "reishi mushroom" as it is also known, is used during chemotherapy and radiotherapy to reduce side effects such as fatigue, appetite loss, hair loss, bone marrow suppression and infection and enhance quality of life.

In animal studies, Ganoderma mushroom has been shown to effectively prevent cancer cells from multiplying. These results are comparable to those of Lentinan. Ganoderma mushrooms have also been said to have a healing effect on the lungs and are particularly beneficial for individuals with asthma and other respiratory problems. An experiment in China showed that when more than 2,000 patients with chronic bronchitis were administered Ganoderma mushroom within two weeks, 60% to 90% showed marked improvement in health.

The Natural Choice

Research has proven that nothing comes close to eating wholesome plant foods to prevent diseases. Not all of the nutrients available in plant foods can be mimicked in a lab and bottled into pills. In fact, fiber and some phytochemicals can only be found in plant foods.

Experts like the US Food and Drug Administration have long advised that we should obtain the variety of nutrients we need from our diet. What we need are healthier food choices — not more pills.

Antioxidants, phytochemicals and polysaccharides offer unlimited hope in the fight against chronic diseases. In fact, statistics show that at least one-third of cancers can be prevented if we eat a balanced diet and exercise often. Now that is food for thought.

Nutritional Immunology
& A Healthy Life

Chapter 8 Your Nutritional Treasure Houses

Many of us prefer to spend hundreds if not thousands of dollars a year on vitamin supplements that can cause us harmful side effects.

This is unnecessary since Mother Nature offers us a treasure-trove of inexpensive, safe, wholesome and disease-fighting foods like fruits, vegetables and herbs.

The list of beneficial plant foods in nature may be endless. However, a visit to your neighborhood vegetable or fruit store will still reveal a convenient source of some amazing plant foods.

Use this chapter as a guide to which plant foods are excellent choices for preparing a delicious and nutritious meal.

1. The Vegetable Market

Alfalfa

Alfalfa may be used in salads, sandwiches and omelets or eaten as a snack. As it is easy to grow and prepare for edible use, it is sometimes called "the father of all foods." Alfalfa contains plant proteins and vitamins. It has therapeutic benefits. It has been said that when some animals fall ill, they will automatically begin foraging for wild alfalfa.

All parts of alfalfa are nutritious and contain protein, fat, the vitamins A, C, E, B_1, B_2, K and fiber, calcium, iron and potassium. It also contains isoflavonoid phytoalexins. The plant can be used to treat fever, scurvy, constipation, urinary tract infections and bad breath. The leaf has been said to be able to prevent heart attack, stroke and cancer as well as reduce blood cholesterol.

Asparagus

Asparagus is a perennial plant that requires special cultivation. Early in the spring, its sprouts can be harvested and eaten, while later in the season, the flowers may be consumed like corn on a cob. Even the pollen can be mixed with other food.

Asparagus is rich in protein, fiber and vitamins like B_1, B_2 and C. Asparagus can nourish the kidneys and urinary tract and cleanse the digestive system. Recently, experts have begun using asparagus to treat rheumatism and edema caused by heart failure.

Barley And Rice

Grown throughout the world, barley and rice are even worshipped for their nutritional value. Due to anti-inflammatory properties, they are often recommended for individuals recovering from illness.

Barley and rice are high in vitamins B and E, protein, carbohydrates and minerals. These plants are sometimes used to treat individuals with loss of appetite and women suffering from nursing discomfort.

Bitter Melon

Bitter melon or bitter gourd tastes bitter because it contains alkaloids. People who try it for the first time will find it bitter. However, its bitterness has been largely reduced with improved techniques in cultivation. In fact, a light, sweet taste will normally replace the initial bitterness. The slight bitterness can stimulate production of saliva and gastric juices, which promote digestion and improve appetite.

Every part of the bitter melon, including the seed, leaf, vine and fruit, has healing effects in traditional medicine. Bitter melon helps treat abdominal discomfort and skin problems. Traditionally, bitter melon is used to allay heat, reduce fatigue, improve vision and tonify the 'qi'. Now, bitter melon is commonly used to strengthen the immune system and help lower blood sugar.

Broccoli

Broccoli belongs to the same family as cauliflower and is sometimes referred to as a doctor for the poor. Broccoli is ranked as one of the top 10 nutritious foods by Time Magazine.

Broccoli contains protein, niacin and the vitamins A and C. Broccoli is one of the richest sources of antioxidants and also contains the phytochemical sulforaphane, which helps lower risk of cancer. Studies have also shown that a broccoli-rich diet can prevent prostate cancer.

Carrot

The wild carrot may be found growing almost anywhere, including along roadsides and meadows in temperate North America and Europe. Carrot has been used as both food and medicine since the 16th century. As a medicine, it was boiled for use as a diuretic and to help dissolve kidney stones.

The entire carrot can be used for medicinal purpose. Carrot can eliminate gas and intestinal worms and improve womb diseases. In modern medicine, the carrot plays an important role in the diet of cancer patients. Carrots contain a lot of fiber, retinoids, beta carotene potassium and the vitamins A, B and C.

Ginger

Ginger, which comes from India, is one of the most commonly used spices in the world. Ancient cultures used it to preserve food and combat digestive problems. Indians believe that ginger possesses healing powers and sometimes use it in religious ceremonies. Chinese sailors used ginger to relieve seasickness while the Greeks wrapped ginger in bread, a concept similar to the modern day gingerbread.

Ginger contains various amino acids, vitamins and other nutrients, which can alleviate migraines, fight ulcers and nourish the respiratory and digestive systems. It is also effective in controlling cholesterol and cleansing the kidneys.

Luffa

Luffa is shaped like a cylinder or wooden club and its size depends on the species. Luffa has a green exterior and soft flesh with black or white shiny seeds. Its tender flesh can be stir fried or boiled in soup.

Luffa contains protein, vitamins and minerals. It can be eaten when young and tender or can be made into medicine when it is old and ripe. Luffa possesses cooling characteristics, can alleviate heat and remove phlegm.

Onion

In the Middle Ages, the onion gained popularity for its ability to quench thirst, ease bowel movement and improve urinary function.

Onions can be manufactured into diuretics, antiseptics, and expectorants. Today, they are used to treat skin problems, clear phlegm, lower total blood cholesterol, boost beneficial HDL cholesterol and prevent blood clotting. They are also said to have anti-cancer properties.

Perilla

Perilla, a member of the mint family, is used by many cultures, especially the Japanese. In Chinese medicine, perilla is used as a carminative, stimulant and antinauseant. It also inhibits tumor growth.

Perilla is high in calcium, iron, potassium, riboflavin, niacin, phosphorus, thiamin and protein as well as the vitamins A and C. Perilla is used to relieve headaches, remove phlegm, relieve cold and flu symptoms and reduce the effects of bacterial infection. Research has shown that perilla is especially effective with fever as it has a mild antipyretic effect — the ability to lower body temperature.

Shiitake Mushroom

For many centuries, the Shiitake mushroom has played an important role in traditional Japanese and Chinese cuisine. It is a medicine as well as a food. In recent years, it was found to have anti-cancer abilities.

Shiitake mushroom contains amino acids, which can be converted to vitamin B_2 and D, adenine, choline, tyrosinase and various mineral salts. The polysaccharide Lentinan extracted from the mushroom stimulates the immune system, activates cells and suppresses tumors. Besides lowering blood pressure and blood cholesterol, Lentinan is effective against dermatitis and the hardening of the liver and blood vessels.

For more information on the Shiitake mushroom, please turn to Chapter 7 of this book.

Soy

Over 5,000 years ago, Chinese farmers began cultivating soy, which they called the "yellow jewel". Soy is priceless and can be made into food, oil and milk. Soy is an excellent source of protein for infants and diabetics. Experiments show that soymilk is comparable to cow's milk in terms of nutritional value.

The highly nutritious soy has twice as much protein as meat, four times that of chicken eggs and 12 times that of cow's milk. Besides, it contains calcium, folic acid, fiber, vitamins and phytochemicals. Soy is also low in fat, cholesterol free and high in fiber. Isoflavones, a soy phytochemical, can lower cholesterol and in turn, prevent heart disease. In addition, soy phytoestrogens have been said to relieve menopausal symptoms and help the body to retain calcium. Genistein, a soy isoflavone, has been shown to inhibit cancer.

Winter Melon

Despite its name, winter melon is harvested in summer.

This nutritious plant food contains protein, carbohydrate and fiber as well as vitamin C. The skin, seed, flesh and leaf all contain medicinal properties. Winter melon seeds are chockfull of essential fatty acids. The flesh has a refreshing taste—although it is high in calories, it is low in sodium. Winter melon is said to be effective in preventing heart disease, high blood pressure, nephritis and bloating.

2. The Fruit Store

Apple

The apple was considered by ancient Egyptians to be both food and medicine. You may have heard of the old adage, "An apple a day keeps the doctor away". This could be because the apple is very high in fiber. The pectin in an apple swells when it comes into contact with water, which is why you feel full when you drink water after eating an apple. As it is highly nutritious, the apple is seen as an ideal food for weight control.

The apple contains protein, fat, carbohydrates, various vitamins, minerals and malic acid. Its soluble fiber content regulates and improves bowel functions. Pectin binds with cholesterol to aid the removal of wastes, which in turn lowers blood cholesterol levels. It also binds to the cholesterol found in the gall bladder and discharges it from the body. This helps dilute bile and prevents formation of gallstones.

Banana

Bananas are said to hail from the Himalayas and are one of the oldest fruits known to mankind.

A banana has high nutritional value. It is a natural source of potassium, with a whopping 467 mg per banana. This makes banana a good choice to prevent high blood pressure. A study reported in the Archives of Internal Medicine confirms that high fiber foods like banana help prevent heart disease. Banana contains vitamin B6, magnesium and tryptophan. Vitamin B6 is a natural anti-depressant while magnesium helps relieve anxiety. The amino acid, tryptophan improves the mood. According to the Archives of Opthamology, banana may improve vision by reducing the risk of age-related macular degeneration (ARMD), the main cause of vision loss in older adults.

Grape Seed

Grapes are often preferred for their fruit but research has shown that the seed contains a very potent antioxidant called OPC. OPC is said to be up to 20 times more powerful than vitamin C and up to 50 times more powerful than vitamin E.

The seeds of red grapes are said to be abundant in OPC. OPC protects the body from injuries and delays aging by raising antioxidant activity in the body.

Papaya

The papaya contains an important digestive enzyme called papain, which can break down protein-based food into a digestible state. In its purest form, papain can tenderize lean meat that is as much as 35 times its weight. This is why papaya is prescribed for those who have problems digesting protein. Papain is found most abundantly in the leaves of the papaya tree and in the skin of the unripe papaya fruit.

Papaya leaves are often wrapped around open wounds and ulcerated skin to draw out foreign material and heal the sores. Papaya seeds and honey make a potent herbal concoction that can expel toxins. Papaya is valued by many herbalists as an excellent blood-clotting agent and is recommended for recovery from wounds. Papaya is also an effective treatment for allergies, hemorrhage, burns, constipation and intestinal problems and helps prevent ulcers.

Peach

The peach is one of the most popular fruits in the world. It cannot endure extreme cold but flourishes in warm, temperate climates. Once the peach is ripened, it is important to harvest it immediately to maintain its taste and quality.

The peach tree contains abundant vitamins, minerals and alpha hydroxy acids (AHA). Among fruits, peach contains the highest amount of iron, which is critical for blood production. The leaves are used as a laxative, expectorant and sedative. The seed has high nutritional and medicinal value. It can be used to treat all kinds of gynecological disorders, abdominal pain, abscesses, pemphigus, constipation, insomnia and hypertension. It may be used to combat tuberculosis. The stem is used as an alterative, astringent, demulcent and sedative. The entire peach can be used as an astringent, febrifuge and parasiticide and has mild sedative properties.

Pineapple

The origin of pineapple is much debated but it is said that Christopher Columbus was the first European to taste this juicy fruit. He came across the pineapple during his travels to the island of Guadeloupe in 1493 and dubbed it the "Pine of the Indies".

Every 100 grams of pineapple fruit contains as much as 30 milligrams of vitamin C. Pineapple has high water content. Like papaya, pineapple flesh contains an enzyme that can break down proteins. Therefore, it can tenderize meat and even dissolve blood clots because it is largely proteins that keep blood platelets together.

Strawberry

Most people consider wild strawberry as the best tasting wild berry. A perennial plant, strawberry grows approximately three to six inches high with delicate, white flowers, which usually blossom between the warm months of April and July. As strawberries have experienced such intense breeding and cultivation over the years, planting and harvesting strawberries have become a gardener's art.

Rich in vitamin C, vitamin B-complex, calcium, phosphorus and potassium, the strawberry is an integral player in herbal medicine. The leaves are often boiled and used as an astringent. They may also be used to treat diarrhea, fever, gout, mouth ulcers and gum disease. The boiled roots and leaves can assuage inflammation in the kidneys and bladder as well as relieve heat and pain. In addition, strawberry juice is used as a beauty aid and remedy for sunburns.

Tangerine

Tangerine is a member of the citrus family. It is sweet and sour with juicy and tender flesh. Tangerine can have a lightening effect on the skin.

Tangerine fruit contains many types of nutrients that improve metabolism. The white streaks found on the surface of tangerine flesh contain bioflavonoids, which can prevent high blood pressure and dissolve phlegm. Tangerine peel contains limonene, retinol, carotene, vitamins B and C and can be used to treat indigestion and gas. Recent research has shown limonene to prevent cancer. Tangerine peel is also used as a freshener, expectorant and tonic.

129

3. The Chinese Medicine Store

Cassia Tora

The Chinese call this plant food "jue ming zi," or "bright eyes." The seeds or fruit of Cassia Tora are commonly used in the treatment of eye ailments such as cataracts, conjunctivitis and glaucoma. Cassia Tora is used to clear vision and to ease itchy, red eyes. It is beneficial to the eyes because it also cleanses and refreshes the liver and kidneys. It also relieves headaches.

Extracts of Cassia Tora seeds have been discovered to possess anti-tumor properties. They are also used to treat hypertension and lower blood cholesterol. Due to its ability to lubricate the intestines, it is often used as a remedy for dry or infrequent stools and constipation.

Chinese Angelica Root/Dong Quai

Dong Quai is an ancient and somewhat mysterious herb and has been used in food for thousands of years. As early as 200 AD, it was listed as an herbal remedy in the Chinese Materia Medica: Shen-nong Ben Cao Jing. Dong Quai was later introduced to Europe and became one of the prescribed herbs for the plague.

Dong Quai is often called the "queen of herbs". It has vitamins A, B12 and E. Vitamin E has a relaxing effect on the central nervous system, and is able to dissolve blood clots and loosen tight muscles. It also helps to improve blood circulation due to its unique ability to clear blood. The seeds and roots of Dong Quai contain essential oils such as phellandrene, alpha pinene, limonene, osthol, angelicin, umbelliferone, bergatpen and psorlene. These oils have been found to be a remedy for diarrhea, dysentery, gonorrhea and syphilis. In Chinese medicine, Dong Quai helps nourish the female body, regulate monthly menstruation and relieve menopausal symptoms. In addition, Dong Quai has been found to exhibit anti-inflammatory effects and can be used to combat allergies.

Chinese Dates

Dates are one of man's best health foods. A tiny date has numerous nutrients. Dates have been planted for over 3,000 years in China. Some popular types of dates are red dates, black dates and honey dates.

Date pulp contains protein, fats, sugar, carotene, riboflavin and ascorbic acid. Its vitamin content is higher than that of tangerines. Dates are valuable since the fruit, root and tree bark can be made into medicines. The highly nutritious fruit nourishes the stomach, spleen and blood. The tender leaf is high in vitamin C and can be made into a drink. The more commonly used dates are red dates. Studies found that red dates could increase oxygen content in the blood and nourish entire body cells. The black date has the ability to nourish the kidneys and blood.

Cinnamon

Cinnamon, a commonly used household spice, comes from an evergreen tree with tiny white and yellow flowers. From China, this precious spice found its way into the hands of the Egyptians, who used it in their famed embalming methods.

Cinnamon contains potassium, calcium, iron and manganese. Manganese acts as an antioxidant in the body. Besides being a natural preservative, cinnamon is used to alleviate nausea, indigestion and vomiting. Cinnamon can also be used as a natural antiseptic since it contains eugenol, which has been known to relieve pain. It has the ability to lower blood pressure and blood cholesterol, treat gynecological disorders, improve skin infections, strengthen the blood and increase energy and immunity.

Ginseng

Ginseng has long been considered the "king of herbs" throughout the world. Ginseng's prominence is evident in early Chinese history. It was included in the first great Chinese herbal encyclopedia, Pen Tsao Ching (The Classic of Herbs), as an herb used for "enlightening the mind and increasing wisdom."

Ginseng is highly nutritious as it contains vitamins A and E, niacin, calcium, iron, potassium and a rare phytochemical called ginsenoside. It strengthens the entire body by increasing the efficiency of the endocrine, metabolic, circulatory and digestive systems. In fact, tests have shown that ginseng can actually prevent cancer cells from developing. Ginseng is considered a tonic for the blood. It can lower blood pressure to normal levels and even reduce cholesterol. Furthermore, chewing the ginseng root is reported to reduce the risk of cardiovascular disease. Ginseng is often used to alleviate other ailments such as stress and fatigue.

Hawthorn

There are about 900 different species of hawthorn shrub. The hawthorn shrub is one of the most beautiful in the world. It traditionally blooms from April to June. It is viewed as a plant that is highly beneficial to the heart.

Hawthorn is high in vitamins B-complex and C. Its berries are used to treat insomnia, nervousness, high cholesterol, heart disease, indigestion and gas. They can also alleviate abdominal distention, kidney problems and sore throat. Hawthorn has the ability to dilate the coronary arteries, which in turn improves blood flow to the heart. It has also been found to be good for all types of heart-rhythm disorders as it is able to regulate the heart's ability to pump.

Licorice

Licorice is recorded in many of the oldest and most respected herbal writings, including Pen Tsao Ching (The Classic of Herbs). Chinese physicians often prescribed licorice for patients suffering from sore throats, coughs, malaria, food poisoning and some cancers. Licorice can also alleviate respiratory, gastrointestinal and genitourinary problems. Interestingly, licorice ranks second only to ginseng as the most important herb in Chinese pharmacology.

Licorice exhibits anti-inflammatory and anti-arthritic properties. It helps to strengthen the immune system by increasing interferon production. It has the ability to fight viruses, specifically the virus that causes Herpes simplex. Licorice is 50 times sweeter than sugar and even a small amount adds tremendous flavor to any herbal formulation.

Lovage

In Chinese literature, the lovage root first appeared in the Divine Husbandman's Classic of Materia Medica where it was recommended for alleviating pain such as headaches, toothaches and stiff neck. Lovage is grown throughout the world. As lovage has a special fragrance, it is used as a spice in sauces and soups. The root may be grated and added to salads.

In many European countries, lovage root is the principal ingredient in several diuretic teas. Lovage is used to treat gastric problems and irritation of the respiratory tract. It is also used to improve blood circulation and treat baldness. Lovage seeds have been known to reduce water retention and help eliminate toxins.

Sterculia Seed

Sterculia seed has been shown to lower blood pressure. Brown and wrinkled in appearance and sweet and cold in nature, sterculia seed contains bassorin, arabinose and galactose. Sterculia seed is traditionally used to soothe sore throat, phlegm and cough but also helps clear the intestines and improve bowel function.

Sterculia seed can act as a diuretic. It helps reduce inflammation, swelling and stops bleeding of the eyes and nose.

4. Rare And Precious Food

Agaricus Blazel Murill (ABM) Mushroom

The ABM mushroom thrives in the humid climate of Sao Paulo, Brazil. Furumoto, a Japanese immigrant living in Brazil, discovered that the locals rarely experienced geriatric diseases or cancer because the ABM mushroom was an integral part of their daily diet.

The ABM mushroom has higher concentration of polysaccharides than any other mushroom. Not only is it used to fight cancer but is also employed as an anti-viral agent. While polysaccharides found in most fungi can only affect certain solid tumors, those in ABM mushroom are effective against Ehrich's ascites carcinoma (EAC), sigmoid colonic cancer, ovarian cancer, breast cancer, lung cancer and liver cancer as well as most solid tumors.

For more information on the ABM mushroom, please turn to Chapter 7 of this book.

Bee Pollen

Bee pollen is the powdery substance from the male plant's stamen. The size and color of the bee pollen varies with the plant species. Bee pollen has a long history as a food and medicine. The Chinese book, "Shen-nong Ben Cao Jing", categorizes bee pollen as a food that can strengthen the body and prolong life. In Chinese palaces, bee pollen used to be made into paste for healing and beauty purposes.

Bee pollen contains large amounts of aspartic acid, an amino acid that has also been known to stimulate the glands and create a feeling of physical rejuvenation. Besides strengthening the immune system, bee pollen has a healing effect on pernicious anemia and disturbances of the intestinal system such as colitis and chronic constipation. In addition, bee pollen has been known to delay the aging process and to increase emotional well being. It normalizes intestinal activities, and improves appetite and fitness levels.

Cactus

Cactus has a long history of use as food. Despite its prickly exterior, cactus has soft and succulent flesh and is very rich in phytochemicals and minerals.

The processing of cactus for food purposes requires great knowledge and skill. It is very important that the right species and right parts of the cactus are chosen. Within the thick, waxy cuticle of the cactus stem, for example, there is a thick membrane that helps prevent water loss from the cactus. When the membrane is consumed in large amounts, it produces a laxative effect. Once the gel has been isolated from the cactus, it must be filtered to remove impurities and cellulose. It is then processed into liquid form. Upon removal, the gel of the cactus oxidizes rapidly. Therefore, processing must take place as soon as the gel has been extracted from the cactus in order to produce the purest and most delicious extract possible.

In fact, cactus may be the most perfect food in nature. Research shows that when applied to the skin, cactus extract acts as a moisturizer and helps prevent water evaporation from the stratum corneum layer. In doing so, cactus extract may improve the skin's barrier function, an action that over time may prevent the development of fine lines and wrinkles caused by free radical damage. In addition to their moisturizing abilities, the nutrients found in cactus extract provide numerous benefits to the body. The cactus contains large quantities of phytochemicals and high levels of antioxidants, which may enhance the body's immune functions. According to scientific studies, cactus may prove to be a vital key in the prevention of cancer, heart disease, and musculoskeletal disorders. In certain parts of the world, cactus is used as a remedy for non-insulin dependent diabetes patients. Cactus has properties that actually lower blood glucose.

Cactus Fruit

Experiments have shown cactus fruit to have a healing effect on wounds. Scientists found that cactus fruit can promote the proliferation of normal human fibroblasts. Cactus fruit plays a significant role in wound healing both inside the body and on the skin's surface.

Cactus fruit is abundant in phytochemicals and antioxidants. Its antioxidant activity is said to be seven times more powerful than that of vitamin C. Cactus fruit is also high in the vitamins A, B1, B12, D3 and riboflavin. Cactus fruit also promotes skin regeneration and softens the skin.

Coriolus Versicolor Mushroom

Coriolus Versicolor mushroom contains the polysaccharide K (PSK), also known as Krestin, which has exhibited anti-microbial, antiviral and anti-tumor properties. PSK use has seen improvements in patients suffering from stomach cancer, colorectal cancer, non-small cell lung cancer, gastric cancer and leukemia.

Some studies show PSP, a polysaccharide peptide in this mushroom, to be an even more potent anti-cancer and immunological regulator than PSK.

For more information on the Coriolus Versicolor mushroom, please turn to Chapter 7 of this book.

Ganoderma Lucidum Mushroom

The Ganoderma Lucidum mushroom is believed by the Chinese to have mysterious healing powers. In China, this mushroom has been known to promote vitality and longevity.

The Ganoderma mushroom contains carbohydrates, amino acids, protein and triterpene. It is used to treat nervousness, dizziness, insomnia, chronic hepatitis and high cholesterol. The different beta-D-glucans isolated from water and alkali extracts of the Ganoderma exhibit anti-tumor activities. Currently, the Ganoderma mushroom is being used to treat and prevent cancer. In cancer treatment, the Ganoderma mushroom may be used to reduce the side effects of chemotherapy, enhance survival rate, reduce the likelihood of metastasis, improve quality of life and help prevent the recurrence of cancer.

For more information on the Ganoderma Lucidum mushroom, please turn to Chapter 7 of this book.

141

Ginseng Berry

Ancient people believed the ginseng root to have supernatural powers. Ginseng is grown throughout the world but not all varieties are of good quality. Scientists have discovered that the ginseng berry may actually be higher in nutritional value than the root.

Ginseng berry has the ability to increase strength, regulate blood pressure, slow down degeneration of the body, increase metabolism, stimulate the function of the endocrine glands and fight fatigue. Ginseng berry extract is effective in treating diabetes and obesity. Ginsenosides, the nutrients in ginseng, can be found in many parts of the plant including the root, leaf and berry. But different parts of the plant have different pharmacological activities. Ginsenoside Re, which is found in ginseng berry, is a potent anti-diabetic.

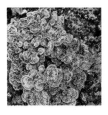

Maitake Mushroom

The effectiveness of the Maitake mushroom is in its polysaccharide content. By refining the constituents in the fruiting body of Maitake mushrooms, scientists were able to extract the D-fraction, the part of polysaccharides that contains potent anti-tumor activities.

Maitake mushroom has been used in protecting healthy cells from becoming cancerous, helping to prevent cancer metastasis, inhibiting tumor growth and reducing the side effects of chemotherapy.

Maitake mushroom is said to reduce the side effects of chemotherapy as it is better tolerated and more effective.

For more information on the Maitake mushroom, please turn to Chapter 7 of this book.

Pearl

For thousands of years, the pearl has been a symbol of beauty, youth and immortality. It was revered by oriental women who used it both externally and internally to preserve their youth.

Pearl is high in nutrients such as vitamin B, polysaccharides, proteins, calcium and nearly 20 types of amino acids. It is often made into a soft paste for clearing rashes and blemishes. It is also effective to heal skin sores and skin ulcers. Other benefits of pearl include anti-inflammatory properties, improvements in vision, stabilization of the nervous system, enhanced removal of toxic substances from body tissues,

143

improvements in skin texture, and strengthening of the bones. Pearl may prevent pigmentation by slowing down the development of melanin. Pearl's high calcium content makes it ideal for bone health.

Royal Jelly

Royal jelly is a substance produced by younger worker bees and fed to the larva from which the queen bee develops. Queen bees live up to eight years, which is 50 times longer than worker bees.

Many studies indicate that royal jelly can prolong life and prevent aging. When royal jelly is added to their diets, athletes have reported increased stamina and general well-being. Royal jelly exhibits anti-inflammatory and anti-bacterial properties.

5. The Herb Garden

Chrysanthemum

Every part of the chrysanthemum is edible. The young leaves have a tangy taste and are often used as flavoring or garnishing for vegetable dishes. The stalks may be cut and stir-fried. Today, as in ancient times, Taoists use the flower heads of the chrysanthemum to make an elixir that is used in their religious ceremonies. Teas made from chrysanthemum have a cooling, antibiotic effect, and can help to reduce blood pressure.

Chrysanthemum is used as an antipyretic and as a treatment for eye ailments, vertigo, abscesses, fainting, headaches, lumbago, and rheumatism. The juice from the leaves is often applied to wounds to alleviate swelling and pain. The flowers, which contain carotenoids and yellow luteolin glucoside, are used to treat boils, carbuncles, dizziness, fever and conjunctivitis. They have a powerful effect on cancerous sores, mammary carcinoma and tumors.

Honeysuckle Flower

The sweet-tasting honeysuckle flower has the ability to cleanse the blood and liver, and is traditionally used to kill germs and remove toxins. Other uses include treating sore throats, fever, rashes and all sorts of skin problems.

Honeysuckle can be used to suppress pathogenic bacteria such as Salmonella typhi, Pseudomonas aeruginosa, Staphylococcus aureus and Streptococcus pneumoniae. It has been shown to have antiviral activity and is effective against severe cases of pneumonia and other infectious diseases.

Jasmine

Jasmine has a fragrance loved by many. In Asia, jasmine is added to desserts and teas for its scent. For centuries, jasmine has been a remedy for common ailments. For instance, the Japanese use jasmine tea to soothe the eyes and skin while in India, it is used to treat poisonous snakebites. It is also used to relieve the nervous system, muscle spasms, dysentery-induced abdominal pain and hepatitis.

Research shows that jasmine can successfully inhibit carcinogenesis caused by nitrosamines. Jasmine has aromatherapeutic effects. Studies show that memory can be enhanced by the scent of the jasmine during learning and relearning sessions.

Lotus

The lotus flower was once used in Egyptian religious ceremonies to promote fertility and immortality. Although it has been appreciated mainly for its beauty, it also offers medicinal properties.

Lotus root contains abundant calcium, phosphorus, iron, carbohydrates and various vitamins. Its vitamin C content is equivalent to that of tangerines. Ancient Chinese herbal remedies recommend lotus for delaying aging and repairing the body. The entire lotus plant can be used to help reduce body fat and treat fever, irritability and diarrhea. Lotus stalks and roots were used to treat acne, eczema and nausea while the seeds were used for heart ailments, sunstroke and reduction of fever.

Mulberry

The mulberry family contains more than 55 genera and 1,000 species. Some species of mulberry leaves are the principal food of the silk worm. Mulberry became increasingly popular as silk products were gradually introduced to all parts of the world. In addition to using mulberry leaves in the process of making silk, the Chinese also make use of all parts of the tree including the bark, leaves, twigs and berries to make medicine.

147

Mulberry leaves are high in protein, vitamins A, B-complex, C, D and E, and 15 essential amino acids. They are used to treat health ailments such as high blood pressure, extreme blood sugar levels, dizziness, vertigo, cramps and spasms. They are also effective for the endocrine system, headaches, bloodshot eyes, coughing and sore throat.

Peppermint

It is an ancient tradition to take peppermint after a meal. People used to suck a stick of peppermint at the end of a meal to aid digestion. In Greek and Roman societies, peppermint was used to preserve food and promote digestion.

The refreshing scent of peppermint has a calming effect. For many centuries, Chinese physicians have used peppermint to treat gas, cough and fever. Peppermint also aids the healing of wounds, burns and insect bites. Peppermint also stimulates bile secretion and helps ulcers to heal. Many stomach or ulcer medicines today include peppermint as an ingredient to soothe the stomach wall and digestive tract.

Psyllium Husk

Psyllium husk contains aucubine, enzymes, fats and mucilage. A natural source of fiber, psyllium husk has the ability to absorb water several times its weight and become a gelatinous mass, which adds water and volume to the feces. With higher water content than other fibers, psyllium husk can soften the feces and prevent constipation.

In Europe and America, psyllium husk is commonly added to high fiber breakfasts for extra fiber. Psyllium husk can promote bowel movement and lower the risk of colon cancer and intestinal diseases. It can also reduce blood cholesterol levels, control the rise of blood sugar levels as well as prevent heart disease and diabetes.

Rose

Rose has a high concentration of valuable nutrients. It has long been used as a beauty enhancer. Besides that, it can enhance stomach function, relieve feminine health problems and help improve circulation.

The rose provides essential nutrients and antioxidants including ascorbic acid, niacin and various vitamins. Besides improving the skin's texture and appearance, rose helps prevent DNA damage, promotes wound healing and encourages phagocytic activity. The rose is edible. Its cherry-like fruits contain 50 times more vitamin C than the lemon. This high concentration of vitamin C helps enhance the production of collagen and protect the body from harmful UV rays.

Section 4

Getting It Right

Nutritional Immunology
& A Healthy Life

Chapter 9 Internal Intelligence

Inside our body is an extraordinary network of different systems. Each system has its own unique function — a function that cannot be replaced or carried out by another system. However, these different systems are interrelated and we need each to be healthy and well nourished to achieve optimal health.

Our main internal systems include the integumentary system (comprising our skin and related tissues), the respiratory system, the digestive system, the circulatory system, the musculoskeletal system, the reproductive system, the endocrine system, the nervous system and the immune system.

To ensure our well being, these systems must work very closely together. Each time our body fights an illness, it will need the combined strengths of all systems to ensure that invaders do not get the upper hand. Hence, we should eat to nourish all of these systems to ensure proper balance and continued health.

A Systematic Strategy

Our body is an amazing creation made up of highly intelligent systems, organs and cells that work in a complex but harmonious relationship. When we eat a balanced diet, exercise as often as we can and get enough rest, we give these powerful protectors the fuel and strength they need to keep us perpetually healthy.

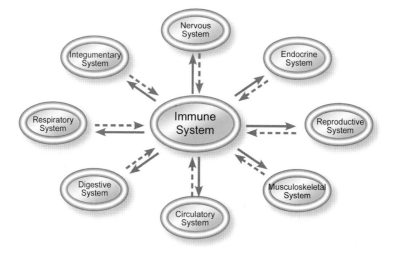

The intimate relationship between the immune system and other systems helps keep us healthy and can prolong life

Our body is like a well-oiled machine. For optimal health, all of its systems must work together — a defect in any one system can sorely compromise our well-being. Just as there is no replacement for the immune system, it is impossible to assume that an artificially created circulatory system or digestive system can perform as well as the one nature has blessed us with.

It cannot be stressed enough therefore, that a healthy, well-nourished body can enhance the workings of our internal systems and in turn, give us a long and productive life.

1. The Integumentary System (Skin)

Your Self-Check Chart

Ask yourself...	Yes	No
Does your skin look dull and lack elasticity?		
Is it blemished or affected by acne?		
Do you suffer from hair loss?		
Do you easily get eczema or tinea?		
Do you suffer from itching hands or athlete's foot?		
Do you suffer from endocrine problems?		
Are you often exposed to the sun?		
Do you frequently suffer from allergies or food poisoning?		
Do you always go to bed late?		

The skin is the body's largest organ. It occupies more than 20 square feet of space and weighs a full 10 pounds. The skin is our first barrier against the millions of potentially harmful substances the body is exposed to daily. Without its tough system of layers, the body's life-sustaining organs and systems would be exposed to an unstoppable barrage of pathogens. Without the skin, the immune system would be easily outnumbered and overwhelmed.

The skin is composed of many layers to provide a series of obstacles to potential invaders.

The top layer is called the epidermis. It covers a thicker layer called the dermis, which houses hair follicles, blood vessels, sweat glands and sebaceous glands. The skin offers both active and passive aid to the immune system. Keeping out potentially harmful microbes by secreting lysosomes and other chemicals is just one of the skin's many active defenses.

The skin's passive defense is its constant process of regeneration where bacteria are discarded together with dead skin cells. Though usually invisible to the naked eye, this process is one of the most important activities of the skin. Every time we scrub our skin or even brush it against another surface, we aid the process of regeneration.

The skin is also a defender in other ways. Its melanin pigment protects us against the sun's damaging rays. The thick dermal layer combines with underlying fat cells to act as a shock-absorbent cushion against external physical contact, further protecting the rest of the body for example, when we fall or are hit by another object.

This system also notifies the immune system of the type of invaders that escape its defenses. The skin's Langerhans cells reveal the identity of foreign substances entering the body through the skin. On receiving this information, the immune system is able to launch an appropriate counter-offensive against the invaders.

2. The Respiratory System

Your Self-Check Chart

Ask yourself...	Yes	No
Do you frequently sneeze when seasons change?		
Do you smoke?		
Do you have genetic diseases such as asthma?		
Do you snore?		
Do you often have difficulty breathing?		
Do you live in a city?		
Do you often have phlegm in your throat?		
Do you suffer from a persistent cough?		
Do you often suffer from a blocked nose?		
Is there any blood when you clear your nose?		

Though it may look simple, the act of breathing is one of the most essential activities of the body. At the same time, it is the function that is most often responsible for pathogens to enter our body. We are fortunate, however, that the respiratory system is well equipped to prevent these pathogens from reaching the lungs.

The respiratory tract is composed of the nose, throat, trachea and bronchial tubes. This set up makes it difficult for invaders to reach the lungs. For example, the curving nasal passage creates a shifting air stream that hinders invaders from entering the respiratory tract. The mucous along the nasal cavity is designed to catch and expel invaders from the system. Invaders who still manage to bypass these defenses must deal with the tonsils and adenoids, which trap and destroy foreign substances. Beyond these organs lie the trachea and bronchial tubes that are lined with mucous

membranes to catch more persistent particles. Trapped particles are then swept out of the respiratory tract by fine, hair-like structures called cilia. However, these defenses, as intelligent as they may seem, cannot provide complete protection for the body.

Therein lies the importance of immune cells and associate actions. Lysozyme is an enzyme found in the mucous of the respiratory tract. It dissolves the cell walls of bacteria. The respiratory system also produces antibodies that kill bacteria and viruses. The alveolar macrophage is an especially powerful immune cell found in the respiratory system. It stations itself in the lungs and engulfs and destroys substances that find their way past the system's initial defenses.

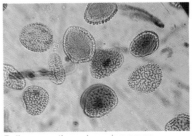

Pollen seen through a microscope

The respiratory system's immune functions help to prevent the risk of airborne diseases that we face every day. Sometimes, this system's mechanisms can malfunction, especially when we do not eat a balanced diet. One example of a system malfunction is respiratory allergies, which occur when our immune cells mistake a harmless substance for a more dangerous threat. When the immune system tries to expel these substances from the respiratory tract, we experience symptoms similar to that of the common cold—sore throat, coughing, sneezing and runny nose.

159

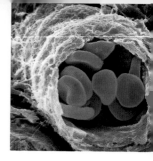

3. The Digestive System

Your Self-Check Chart

Ask yourself...	Yes	No
Do you often have gastric pain?		
Do you frequently suffer from constipation or diarrhea?		
Do you frequently have flatulence?		
Do you suffer from hemorrhoids?		
Do you suffer from excessive internal heat or halitosis?		
Do you have poor appetite?		
Do you consume a lot of alcoholic drinks?		
Do you feel stressed very often?		
Do you follow a regular diet, work and rest routine?		

The digestive system houses a series of defenses similar to that of the respiratory system. The mouth, esophagus, stomach and intestines all take part in the complex process of breaking down food and distributing energy and nutrients to various parts of the body. However, this same food can contain potentially harmful and even lethal microbes.

Lysozyme in our saliva is designed to kill harmful bacteria that enter the mouth. Macrophages, our scavenging immune cells, patrol the entrance to the digestive tract. The digestive tract is also lined with thick mucous membranes to trap foreign substances. Trapped substances are then driven from the body through a wave-like motion called peristalsis. The stomach lining secretes hydrochloric acid, one of the most corrosive of chemicals, to kill bacteria on contact.

In addition, beneficial organisms that live in the digestive tract provide protection against hostile substances in exchange for nutrients. However, even these beneficial organisms can pose a risk for those with a compromised immune system. E. coli, candida and other strains of bacteria that live harmoniously within the body can turn deadly if the immune system becomes weak due to stress, injury or an improper diet. These normal organisms, no

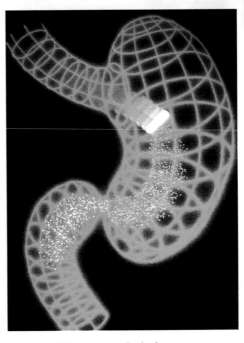

longer kept in check by the body's natural defenses, can invade surrounding tissues and multiply out of control.

The digestive system must be treated with proper care to maintain its delicate balance and ability to defend the body. The digestive system is particularly affected by the food we eat and as such, a healthy diet is essential to its immune functions.

4. The Circulatory System

Your Self-Check Chart

Ask yourself...	Yes	No
Does heart disease and high blood pressure run in your family?		
Do you often have cold hands and feet?		
Do you often experience tingling in your hands and feet?		
Do you feel dizzy when you stand up after sitting for a long time?		
Do you eat a lot of high-fat meat?		
Do you consume a lot of alcoholic drinks?		
Do you exercise regularly?		
Do you have high blood pressure?		
Do you have high cholesterol and triglycerides?		
Do you smoke?		
Are you overweight?		

The circulatory system is an elaborate network made up of thousands of miles of veins, arteries and capillaries. Thanks to a steadily pumping heart, this system forces blood to every organ. The blood vessels not only deliver oxygen and nutrients to all parts of the body but also act as a transportation network for immune cells.

White blood cells in the form of lymphocytes, phagocytes, neutrophils and macrophages patrol the arteries in search of invaders. At any given moment, a trillion or more lymphocytes and other immune cells defend the body. Powered by the pumping heart, these cells flow through every branch of the circulatory network. Some flow freely in the bloodstream while others attach to vessel walls or pass into outlying tissues to fight harmful cells.

However, to function smoothly, the circulatory system must be well nourished to keep veins and arteries free of interfering substances such as cholesterol.

5. The Musculoskeletal System

Your Self-Check Chart

Ask yourself...	Yes	No
Do your joints ache when the weather changes?		
Do you use the computer for long periods of time?		
Does your back often hurt?		
Have you ever received any bone injuries?		
Do you tend to strain your muscles and joints when exercising?		
Do you have difficulty with certain actions such as squatting?		
Do you experience discomfort when carrying heavy items?		
Do you take medicines containing adrenal cortical hormones and thyroid hormones?		

Our inner skeletal structure is made up of a complex grouping of bones, ligaments, tendons and muscles. This strong, basic structure houses our delicate organs and physiological systems. As such, the musculoskeletal system must be well cared for through regular exercise and a healthy diet.

Bones also house critical immune functions. Deep within them lies the bone marrow, which creates red blood cells and white blood cells. The latter are the soldiers of the immune system. Every second, about eight million blood cells die and the same number are regenerated.

Therefore, without a diet rich in calcium and other bone-strengthening nutrients, the body can be gravely compromised. When properly nourished however, our white blood cells will flow freely from the marrow to constantly rejuvenate the immune system.

6. The Reproductive System
Your Self-Check Chart

Ask yourself...	Yes	No
Are you pregnant?		
Has your ability to have intercourse declined?		
Do you have satisfactory intercourse?		
Is your vagina (female) / semen (male) in a healthy condition?		
Do you practice good personal hygiene?		
Do you experience any unknown discharge from your reproductive organ?		
Have you ever had any surgery of the reproductive organ?		
Is there any foul odor from your vagina (female)?		
Do you have to use the restroom frequently?		
Do you have more than one sexual partner?		

One of the greatest miracles of the human race is our power to create new life. The human reproductive system must be protected at all cost because it is responsible for our very existence. Because of this, the defenses of the reproductive system, especially the female, are some of the toughest in the body.

Infectious organisms that enter a woman's body through the reproductive tract are met by a well-organized system of defenses. The reproductive tract is lined with mucous secreted by the vaginal lining. This mucous contains both acid and immune cells to kill most bacteria and other invaders. Tiny, waving cilia brush intruders out of the

tract and create currents to sweep out most pathogens from this area. Antibodies monitoring the reproductive tract destroy the more persistent pathogens.

As the body labels all cells with simple "self" and "non-self" markers, sperm are also subjected to this treatment. That's why of the 200 to 500 million sperm that enter a woman's reproductive tract, over 100 million are destroyed on contact; only about a thousand reach the uterus and only a few hundred reach the fallopian tubes.

A fertilized egg is also attacked by this protection system. As an embryo contains genetic material from the mother and the father, the mother's immune system labels it as a non-self and produces antibodies to attack it. The placenta forms to bridge the mother's self-preservation function and the unborn infant's immune system. The placenta is tissue that connects the infant's umbilical cord to the uterus and filters oxygen and nutrients from the mother's blood to the fetus. This semi-permeable barrier locks out the mother's hostile antibodies and lets in beneficial antibodies for protection.

With all these obstacles, it is indeed a miracle that human life continues. These defenses are critical to the health of the body and when not well taken care of, that is, through a balanced diet, the reproductive system may not be able to protect us against life-threatening illnesses.

7. The Endocrine System

Your Self-Check Chart

Ask yourself...	Yes	No
Do you frequently suffer from long, irregular, or painful periods?		
If you're experiencing menopause, are your symptoms severe?		
Are you over-worked or have little energy?		
Are you abnormally fat or thin?		
Do you easily get nervous?		
Are you very emotional?		
Are you easily depressed?		
Do you have difficulties concentrating for long periods of time?		
Do you often consume stimulants like coffee and tea?		
Do you feel sluggish even when talking?		

The endocrine system is responsible for producing the chemicals and hormones needed by the body to regulate its integrated systems. The endocrine system comprises specialized tissues and organs, including the pituitary, thyroid and adrenal glands, as well as the hypothalamus, pancreas, ovaries and testes. Each of these glands and organs secretes hormones that control a part of the body's functions. Hormones come in various forms and regulate processes like reproduction, growth, metabolism and cell repair. As hormones are released into the blood according to the need of a particular system, stress and infection can cause hormone levels to rise or fall.

The endocrine system acts as a communication line between the brain and the immune system. Immune cells manufacture hormones that allow the immune system to coordinate its activities with the other systems. For example, corticosteroids are hormones produced by the adrenal glands to regulate mood, sleep patterns, muscle strength and the metabolism of carbohydrates, protein and fat. Corticosteroids help regulate these daily bodily functions as well as provide emergency support in cases of infection and disease.

When we are placed in a stressful situation, whether real or imagined, the entire body responds by flooding the blood stream with corticosteroids. At this moment, the immune and digestive systems will come to a halt while our muscles will be strengthened to enhance physical performance. While this strategy was essential for the survival of our prehistoric forefathers, it can today, be very harmful for the immune system. Modern day stresses are more emotional in nature with less need for physical confrontations. When such stressful emotions continue, corticosteroids accumulate, further suppressing the immune system and letting the body become prone to illness.

The best solutions to this dilemma are eating a balanced diet, exercising regularly and giving ourselves healthy outlets for stress.

8. The Nervous System

Your Self-Check Chart

Ask yourself...	Yes	No
Do you often have migraine headaches?		
Do you have poor memory?		
Do you have bouts of insomnia?		
Do you have problems concentrating or trouble thinking clearly?		
Do you suffer from any psychiatric disorders?		
Are you unable to sit still for long periods of time?		
Do your arms and legs easily ache?		
Do you sometimes have difficulty walking stably or difficulty moving your limbs?		
Do you experience unexplained changes in body temperature, appetite or preferences?		
Have you ever felt dizzy or faint without knowing the cause?		

The nervous system is literally the nerve center of all the other systems. The nervous system comprises the brain, spinal cord, nerves and neurons (nerve cells).

One of the key responsibilities of the nervous system is to regulate immune function. Nerve fibers lead from the brain stem and spinal cord to the thymus, where immune cells receive specialized training. Neural pathways connect the brain to the immune system, and the mind coordinates immune function through chemical and electrical signals. Through these channels, the nervous system has the power to spur immune cells into action when the body is under attack. This same process orders the immune cells to stop fighting once the infection is defeated.

The brain's influence on immune function can also be psychological. Studies show that having a cheerful mindset can reduce visits to the doctor by 50% indicating that the immune system of people who think positively is stronger. In the same way, a negative approach to life has been shown to interfere with immune function.

Nutritional Immunology
& A Healthy Life

Chapter 10 Drug Fact And Fiction

Recent medical advancements have brought mankind a false sense of security. Medicine is viewed as a safe substance that can quickly treat illnesses. Many do not realize the harm that can accompany such treatment. Unfortunately, a side-effect free treatment is a rarity. And once the immune system is damaged, the road to recovery is a long and difficult one.

Only the immune system knows exactly how, when and where to take appropriate action to resolve our illness, pain or fatigue. Unlike the immune system, drugs can only achieve a single purpose, such as stimulating the immune system or suppressing it. Drugs are also very often accompanied by harmful side effects. Sometimes, these side effects are even more dangerous than the conditions that demand treatment.

1. Multivitamins

Can Vitamin Pills Cause Harm?

Many of us lead busy lives with little time to eat balanced meals. As such, we assume that by popping a multi-vitamin pill, we've made up for what we lack. We think that even if these pills do not help us, at least they will not harm us.

Moreover, as vitamin labels usually list the US Recommended Daily Allowance (RDA) of vitamins and minerals, we assume the pill contains an ideal dose.

This assumption is flatly refuted by experts like the US Food and Drug Administration (FDA) and the British Food Standards Agency (FSA). The FDA and FSA advise that popping such pills regularly could do serious harm to the body.

The RDA, established by the American Food and Nutrition Board, only acts as a nutritional guideline. It represents the maximum recommended vitamin and mineral need of an adult male on a 2,000 calorie diet. According to nutritionists, it was developed to reverse nutrient deficiency symptoms. So for the average person, the RDA could represent values much higher than his or her actual need.

RDA values also change and it is important to know how much you are taking. For example, the daily RDA for vitamin A used to be a maximum of 5,000 international units (IU) but today, this figure has been revised to a much lower 3,000 IU a day for men and 2,330 IU a day for women.

Too much vitamin A can cause fatigue while an excess of vitamin B6 can affect the nervous system. Too much vitamin A or just five times the RDA of vitamin D can damage the liver.

Aware of the dangers of overdosing on vitamin pills, the American Association of Pediatrics warns against giving infants vitamin supplements as it could increase their risk of getting allergies or asthma.

Vitamin C

Many vitamin C pills contain 250 milligrams of the vitamin or more. People take high-potency vitamin C pills thinking that they will be protected against colds and infections. But the US National Academy of Sciences advises men to take only 90 milligrams of the vitamin a day and women, just

173

75 milligrams. A healthy body absorbs only about 200 milligrams of vitamin C and the surplus is carried away by the urine.

Thus far, there is no conclusive evidence to say that a large dose of vitamin C can prevent or treat the common cold. Researchers only report a mild reduction in the duration of the cold by about half a day. Besides, overdosing on vitamin C can cause alarming side effects.

A study by the University of Pennsylvania has linked too many vitamin C pills with DNA damage. DNA damage can lead to cancer. Says Dr Victor Herbert, an expert on antioxidant use, too much vitamin C can contribute to toxic levels of iron in the blood, leading to cancer and heart disease. Over 1,000 milligrams of vitamin C, 1,500 milligrams of calcium or 17 milligrams of iron a day could also cause abdominal pain and diarrhea.

Vitamin E

In 1994, the New England Journal of Medicine featured a study where beta-carotene pills increased occurrence of lung cancer among heavy smokers in Finland. The journal also reported that test subjects given vitamin E supplements suffered more strokes because vitamin E can interfere with the body's natural blood clotting processes.

Dr Herbert's research has also shown that large doses of vitamin E may promote autoimmune diseases like diabetes, rheumatoid arthritis and multiple sclerosis. In a 1984 report, the National Academy of Sciences warned that elderly Californians on huge doses of vitamin E died 2.3 times earlier than those who did not take supplements.

The FDA also warns that combining vitamin pills with certain prescription drugs could bring about adverse effects. For example, as aspirin and vitamin E both thin the blood, taking them together could increase potential for internal bleeding.

Vitamins are essential for health. They help us in many of our daily bodily functions. However, as cautioned by the American Dietetic Association and the National Academy of Sciences, the best way to obtain our vitamins is through wholesome food. Experts maintain that vitamins in supplement form should not be used as a substitute for a balanced diet.

Vitamins/ Minerals	Large doses could cause
Vitamin A	birth defects; fatigue; skin discoloration; bone pain; liver damage
Vitamin B3	liver damage; peptic ulcers; skin rashes
Vitamin B6	confusion; numbness; unsteadiness; depression
Vitamin C	diarrhea; kidney stones; poisonous levels of iron in the blood, leading to heart and liver problems
Vitamin D	liver damage; calcium deposits that can damage the heart, lungs and kidneys; nausea
Vitamin E	possible slow down in immune function; fatigue; internal bleeding
Iron	poisonous levels of iron in the blood, leading to heart and liver problems; intestinal upset
Calcium	formation of kidney stones; inability of the body to absorb other minerals like iron, manganese and zinc; extreme lethargy

2. Cold Medicines

The effects of the common cold are undoubtedly uncomfortable. Billions of dollars are spent every year on cold related medicines despite knowing that the cold is incurable. Although the effectiveness of some of these medicines is debatable, people still continue to consume them even when side effects are experienced. Many pay a heavy price for short-term relief.

Cold And Allergy Medicines

A cold is caused by a virus. Cold medicines may help suppress symptoms but the virus responsible will continue to roam inside the body.

Despite this, nary a household goes without some form of cold medication in its medicine cabinet. Besides their questionable ability to provide relief, cold medicines may contain drugs such as triprolidine, pseudoephedrine, guaifenesin, phenylpropanolamine and phenylephrine. Many cold medicines combine several of these chemicals into one tablet, giving the false impression that more is better, when in actuality, they may increase the risk of unwanted side effects.

Some damaging effects of these drugs are high blood pressure (making the drugs dangerous for those with heart disease, diabetes or thyroid disease), confusion, nervousness, dry mouth, constipation, difficulty urinating, decreased sweating and worsening of glaucoma.

People also regularly use these medicines to treat allergies. Nasal sprays with ingredients like pseudoephedrine hydrochloride or other antihistamines may prove harmful to allergy sufferers. Using these ingredients could lead to rebound congestion, increased nasal stuffiness and permanent damage to membranes lining the nose.

Cough Suppressants

Just like a runny nose, a cough is actually a way for the body to expel an infection. Although a dry and painful cough may be a sign of a more serious infection, it is generally advised that productive coughs should not be suppressed.

Adverse effects of cough suppressants such as hydrocodone, dextromethorphan and phenyltoloxamine include skin rash, dizziness, nausea, nasal congestion, constipation, dry mouth, difficulty urinating, blurred vision and headache. The combination of iodinated glycerol and codeine, commonly promoted as a cough suppressant, should especially be avoided. An unpublished study performed under the direction of the National Toxicology Program (Department of Human Services) found that iodinated glycerol might cause illnesses as severe as cancer. In general, coughs are most effectively combated by clear liquids, which help thin mucous and promote better breathing.

Antihistamines

Some drugs actually prolong cold symptoms and antihistamines are a prime example of drugs that people think can effectively treat any illness. Antihistamines can make a cold or cough worse by thickening nasal secretions and drying our mucous membranes.

Antihistamines are medicines designed to help stop allergy symptoms such as itching eyes and sneezing. However, they can cause serious side effects like confusion, short-term memory loss, disorientation, dry mouth, constipation and an upset stomach.

The antihistamine, hydroxyzine, used to treat itching and hives, may also cause restlessness, seizures, trembling or shakiness. Diphenhydramine has been known to cause unusually fast heartbeat, increased sensitivity to the sun, unusual bleeding, sore throat, nervousness, restlessness, irritability and ringing in the ears. Although adverse cardiovascular effects are rare, patients have reportedly experienced cardiac arrest, ventricular arrhythmias and even death as a result of using the antihistamine astemizole. You should also tell your doctor if you are taking other prescription medicines as experts say antihistamines could react negatively when taken in combination with other drugs.

Asthma Drugs

Asthma's symptoms may resemble that of the common cold but asthma is a much more delicate condition that needs careful monitoring and treatment.

Drugs such as aminophyllines, theophylline and oxtriphylline are frequently used to treat symptoms of chronic asthma, bronchitis and emphysema, including difficult breathing, sneezing, chest tightness and shortness of breath. Asthma drugs open airways in the lungs and increase air flow, making breathing easier, but there are risks.

The body can only tolerate a specific amount of asthma drugs. Too little may bring on an asthma attack while too much could lead to seizures, irregular heart rhythm and a pounding heartbeat. Adverse effects include bloody stools, confusion, diarrhea, dizziness, flushed skin, headache, increased urination, loss of appetite, muscle twitching, nausea, trembling, trouble sleeping, vomiting of blood and heartburn.

The asthma drug pirbuterol can worsen high blood pressure, diabetes or heart disease. Inhaled drugs, such as albuterol and terbutaline, have been found to cause tremors, jitters, nervousness and in extreme cases, tumors in the ligaments and heart disease.

Antibiotics

Antibiotics are used to treat a diverse range of bacterial infections like pneumonia because they can break down a bacterium's cell walls. But as viruses do not have cell walls, antibiotics are useless against viral infections. However, sometimes, antibiotics are still prescribed to combat the common cold — a viral infection.

In 1983, 51% or more of the three million patients who saw doctors for the common cold were given unnecessary antibiotics. Many people do not realize that using antibiotics to treat viral infections actually worsens the illness. Antibiotics will kill both the good and bad cells. Under these circumstances, antibiotics do not only prove to be useless, but may worsen the problem.

Side effects of antibiotics include allergic reactions, diarrhea, skin rash, abnormal weakness, joint and muscle pain, nausea, vomiting and bleeding. In extreme cases, antibiotics may even cause bone marrow poisoning, seizures, allergic shock or death. In China, antibiotic misuse by both patients and doctors kills about 80,000 people annually.

Researchers warn that misusing antibiotics can affect acquired immunity and lead to potentially dangerous bacterial resistance. For instance, when your child takes antibiotics for Strep throat, the antibiotics replace the immune cells' function in stopping the infection. As the immune cells are not given a chance to fight the bacteria, they do not develop immunity to the bacteria. This can lead to recurring Strep throats. Antibiotics may prove useless against the same bacteria, as it may have already developed resistance to the medicine. Therefore, in some cases, it is better for our body to fight diseases on its own.

The US Food and Drug Administration has expressly warned against the misuse of antibiotics, stating that "bacteria and other microorganisms that cause infections are remarkably resilient and can develop ways to survive the drugs meant to kill or weaken them. This antibiotic resistance, also known as antimicrobial resistance or drug resistance, is due largely to the increasing use of antibiotics."

3. Gastrointestinal Drugs

The average modern diet is an invitation to stomach problems. A diet rich in fat, sugar, salt and calories burdens the digestive system. Choosing drugs instead of good nutrition to calm a troubled stomach can only lead to more harm. Apart from adverse side effects, taking drugs could also promote a habit of making poor dietary choices.

Antacids And Antiflatulents

Antacids are used to treat excess stomach acid and are widely available in neighborhood drug stores. To many people, antacids are considered a simple solution to an upset stomach. But the contents of antacids deserve consideration.

Common ingredients of antacids include aluminum hydroxide, magnesium hydroxide and simethicone. Excess aluminum can damage the bones and magnesium can cause severe diarrhea. Doctors strongly discourage older adults with severe kidney disease from using magnesium-based antacids. Other adverse side effects of antacids include painful urination, dizziness, irregular heartbeat, muscle weakness, vomiting and stomach cramps.

Aluminum hydroxide, magnesium hydroxide and simethicone are also found in antiflatulents (anti-gas) drugs. However, there seems to be no conclusive proof that simethicone, alone or combined with other ingredients,

183

effectively treats excess gas. In fact, experts largely believe that treating excess gas is futile. It is widely agreed that the best method to combat excess gas is to watch what we eat.

Laxatives

Statistics show that Americans spend US$725 million a year on laxatives. As with antacids and antiflatulents, laxatives are consumed more often than they are necessary. This is dangerous for several reasons.

First, laxatives can cause lasting damage to the intestines and can interfere with the body's absorption and use of nutrients. Second, laxatives can be habit forming. If taken for long periods, they inhibit the body's natural ability to digest food properly. Scientists are also discovering other alarming concerns regarding laxatives. For example, the laxative ingredient danthron was recently recalled in the United States because of its cancer-causing properties.

Experts also caution against using laxatives to "clean out the system" or promote intestinal regularity, a process that the body usually controls naturally. In fact, all we need to promote intestinal regularity is a healthy diet filled with wholesome plant foods and plenty of water. Although even the healthy sometimes experience constipation, eating fiber-rich foods like unprocessed bran, whole-grain breads and fresh fruits, drinking a lot of fluids and exercising regularly can help stimulate intestinal activity.

Acid Blockers And Ulcer Drugs

Nizatidine, famotidine, cimetidine and ranitidine are popular stomach acid blockers — drugs used to treat duodenal and gastric ulcers and conditions caused by excess stomach acid like gastroesophageal reflux disease (GERD).

The long-term safety of these drugs remains unknown but harmful side effects may include confusion, hallucinations, dizziness, sore throat and fever, irregular heartbeat, abdominal pain, skin rash, depression, diarrhea, hair loss, headache and nausea. As older people eliminate drugs more slowly from their bodies, they are at an especially high risk of experiencing side effects.

Ulcer drugs such as sucralfate, misoprostol and omeprazole are used to treat ulcers resistant to the usual treatment with stomach acid blockers or antacids. Adverse effects of ulcer drugs include constipation, dizziness, backache, drowsiness, dry mouth, indigestion, stomach cramps, difficulty breathing, fever, cloudy or bloody urine, bleeding or bruising and skin rash. Certain ulcer drugs have also been shown to alter chemical markers of bone metabolism, a risk factor for osteoporosis. Long-term suppression of acid by ulcer drugs can also cause intestinal infections.

Stomach acid blockers and ulcer drugs are by no means solutions for minor digestive complaints such as the occasional upset stomach. They should also not be used by those with pre-existing medical conditions or in combination with other drugs due to the risk of side effects. In addition, an ulcer may still recur despite treatment.

Long term prevention is therefore, a better bet. Those prone to ulcers would benefit from avoiding smoking and foods that are known to trigger ulcers as well as ulcer-aggravating nonsteroidal anti-inflammatory drugs (NSAIDs).

4. Pain Killers

For someone in pain, the idea of immediate relief can be highly tempting. Whether out of desperation or habit, many people turn regularly to pain medications to relieve headaches, back injuries, menstrual pain and other ailments. Pain killers can live up to the promise of quick relief but in turn, they can bring a variety of dangerous consequences. Widely used pain killers include aspirin, NSAIDs and steroidal anti-inflammatory drugs.

Aspirin

Aspirin has become so popular that people think it can treat almost any health dilemma.

According to Basil Hirschowitz MD, a University of Alabama at Birmingham gastroenterologist, "In 30 cases of patients with surgery for intractable ulcers, blood tests showed they had been taking aspirin. But half the patients denied using aspirin. Many people may not realize aspirin is in the medicine they are taking or they are in denial of the potential dangers of taking the drug."

Aspirin is a corrosive substance, which when used for long periods of time or in high doses, can increase our risk of developing peptic ulcers in the lower part of the esophagus, the stomach or the beginning of the small intestine. Aspirin also causes bleeding in the stomach and over time, can weaken the body's ability to slow and contain bleeding throughout the body. Taking aspirin for as little as three days can increase the amount of bleeding during childbirth, tooth extraction and surgery. Many doctors recommend that people with serious liver disease, kidney malfunction, vitamin K deficiency and blood clotting disorders refrain from taking aspirin.

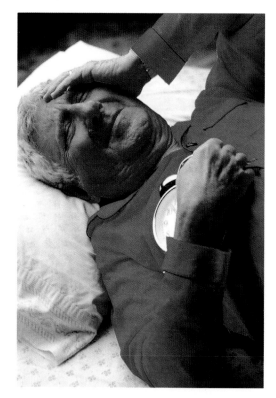

Some people can also be allergic to aspirin and experience rashes or hives, swollen lymph nodes, breathing difficulties, drop in blood pressure or in extreme cases, collapse in shock, after taking it. Children with flu or chicken pox should not be given aspirin as it could cause Reye's syndrome.

Nonsteroidal Anti-Inflammatory Drugs (NSAIDs)

NSAIDs work by stopping the formation of chemicals in the body that cause pain such as headaches, fever, as well as inflammation such as arthritis. Many NSAIDs are available as OTC drugs. Examples of NSAIDs are acetaminophen or paracetamol (found in Panadol and Tylenol), ibuprofen (found in flu pills like Advil and Motrin), mefenamic acid (found in Ponstan) and naproxen (found in Naprosyn).

NSAIDs are widely misunderstood. For example, while numbing pain, acetaminophen does not help stiffness or inflammation. The elderly also tend to consume such pain killers without realizing that their kidneys now have reduced capability to clear these drugs from their system and as a result, they should take a reduced dosage of the drugs. Large doses of acetaminophen may cause liver damage or even death.

Experts advise informing your doctor if you're taking an OTC drug like NSAIDs. Otherwise, taking another prescription drug can be harmful. For example, combining an OTC fever drug containing acetaminophen with a similar prescription drug can be deadly. NSAIDs like mefenamic acid also have a tendency to upset the stomach.

189

The National Consumers League says that over 175 million Americans take OTC tablets to relieve pain without being aware of the dangers. Of the 84% who took pain medications in 2002, 44% admitted exceeding the recommended dose. Surveys indicate that one third of OTC drug consumers don't read the label before buying or using the drug. If you don't have time for drug labels, heed this: 16,500 Americans die each year and 103,000 are hospitalized for NSAID-related complications. NSAID almost triples the risk of stomach bleeding, usually without warning.

Steroidal Anti-Inflammatory Drugs (Steroids)

Steroids are very important hormones that help control inflammation and regulate vital body functions. Arthritis sufferers sometimes switch to steroids if NSAIDs do not provide adequate relief. However, steroids are also associated with various side effects.

Steroids work by suppressing the immune system, making us more vulnerable to infections. Older adults also have a risk of developing osteoporosis as a result of using steroids.

Steroids' side effects are highly dependent on the duration of use. For example, short term use of corticosteroids has been linked with reversible symptoms of hypertension, hyperglycemia, gastrointestinal bleeding, glaucoma, mood disorders, psychotic reactions, pancreatitis, proximal myopathy and sodium and water retention.

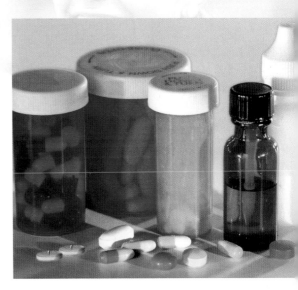

Long term adverse effects include amenorrhea, aseptic necrosis of the bone, cataracts, cushingoid appearance, hypothalamic-pituitary axis suppression, hyperlipidemia, hypertension, mood disorders, muscle weakness and osteoporosis.

5. Psychiatric Drugs

There are many who, desiring optimal health, turn to drug to enhance psychological well being. It was found that many Americans periodically use some form of psychiatric medication such as tranquilizers, sleeping pills, anti-psychotic drugs and anti-depressants, which are widely available on the market. These medicines are used to treat symptoms like anxiety, insomnia, hyperactivity, absent-mindedness and depression. Misguided treatment of these health problems could result in serious repercussions. These medicines should only be used after thorough research and careful evaluation.

Tranquilizers And Sleeping Pills

Today's lifestyle has become synonymous with stress and agitation. Studies show that 15.6% of people use tranquilizers to relieve anxiety. Of this percentage, 39% use these drugs daily and 78% admit to taking tranquilizers for over a year.

Most tranquilizers belong to a chemical family called benzodiazepines with drug names like Valium, Librium, Xanax and Halcium. Sleeping pills belong to another class of tranquilizers from the barbiturates group such as buspirone, diphenhydramine, hydrozyzine and meprobamate.

These drugs are popular but are they really effective? Studies show that most potent tranquilizers are ineffective after about four months of use and sleeping pills have been shown to lose efficacy after just two to four weeks of use. In addition, tranquilizers and sleeping pills can be very dangerous to health.

Side effects include low blood pressure, hip fractures, liver disease and allergies. Mind-altering effects include decreased mental function, forgetfulness, withdrawal syndromes and lack of coordination. Alarmingly, about 16,000 traffic accidents a year are attributed to motorists driving under the influence of such drugs.

Evidence also suggests that tranquilizers are unnecessary as patients have responded as well to placebos in some studies. According to the World Health Organization (WHO), "anxiety is a normal response to stress, and only when it is severe and disabling should it lead to drug treatment."

Anti-psychotic Drugs

Anti-psychotic drugs are meant to treat serious mental illnesses such as schizophrenia, manic-depression and dementia. However, it is said that in the US, an estimated 750,000 people over the age of 65 use these drugs although not all have been diagnosed with such illnesses. Experts believe that many people wrongly turn to anti-psychotic drugs after experiencing symptoms similar to schizophrenia like hallucinations and confusion. In many cases, these symptoms are side effects induced by other drugs that the person takes regularly.

Adverse effects of anti-psychotic drugs include nerve damage, tardive dyskinesia (difficulty chewing or swallowing), loss of balance, muscular fatigue, delirium and Parkinson's disease. One study found that 36% of patients with drug-induced Parkinson's had been taking anti-psychotic drugs when diagnosed with the disease.

The February 2004 issue of the Diabetes Care journal warns that people taking anti-psychotic drugs should be carefully monitored for signs of developing diabetes, obesity or high cholesterol. This warning comes from the American Diabetes Association, the American Psychiatric Association, the North American Association for the Study of Obesity, and the American Association of Clinical Endocrinologists.

Antidepressants

Depression is a serious and very real illness and should not be ignored. It is said to affect over 15 million Americans. But as with many other mental illnesses, its causes and symptoms can be misunderstood.

Depression can actually be caused by drugs used to treat other ailments. Depression could also be triggered by thyroid disorders, cancer, hepatitis or other chronic diseases. It is essential to investigate the underlying causes of depression and understand the detailed history of the patient before treatment is given.

The prolonged and excessive use of some antidepressants have been known to cause low blood pressure, irregular heart rate, enlarged prostate, nausea, blurred vision, excessive thirst, diarrhea, drowsiness, loss of memory, dizziness or muscle weakness.

Whether used to treat simple stress or a more serious mental disorder, psychiatric drugs can have a profound and detrimental effect on both our physical and mental well being. Before taking such a drug, it is imperative to consult a physician to determine its necessity and correct dosage as well as analyze possible consequences.

6. A Healthier Diet, A Better Life

Good nutrition can prevent many diseases and therefore, stop you from having to turn to potentially harmful drugs. Apart from nutrition, it is also important to educate ourselves on factors that can seriously affect our quality of life. With knowledge comes power. Read on and arm yourself with some facts so that you too can make better dietary and lifestyle decisions.

How do antioxidants, phytochemicals and polysaccharides work in harmony to prevent cancer?

Different nutrients prevent different ways in which cancer occurs. Cancer can occur through a variety of means. A cancer may be caused by free radicals. In this case, we need an abundance of antioxidants to help prevent free radical attacks.

Cancer may also be caused by animal hormones, pollution and suppressed immune function. Phytochemicals have been found to help us prevent the causes of cancer.

We constantly come into contact with cancer-causing chemicals, radiation and viral infections. Polysaccharides not only prevent cancer from occurring, but they also destroy existing cancer cells and viruses by increasing the production of interleukin and interferon and by boosting overall cellular immunity.

What are some of the plant foods that are rich in antioxidants, phytochemicals and polysaccharides?

Some nutrient powerhouses include:

Antioxidants: grape seed, cactus fruit, ginseng berry, rose, five leaf ginseng and citrus

Phytochemicals: soy, cactus, broccoli, cauliflower, ginseng berry, chrysanthemum, cassia tora, mulberry leaf and sophora bean

Polysaccharides: pearl, mushrooms like Shiitake, Reishi, Maitake, Coriolus Versicolor and Agaricus Blazel Murill

Should I avoid preserved meats?

The WHO reports that eating large amounts of preserved meat and red meat can increase cancer risk. Experts say that this could be due to nitrites, which are added to many preserved meats to maintain color and to prevent contamination with bacteria. Nitrites can be converted in the stomach to carcinogenic nitrosamines, which may increase the risk of stomach cancer.

Diets high in vegetables and fruits that contain vitamin C and phytochemicals retard the transformation of nitrites to nitrosamines. Some meat preserved through salt or certain acids may also cause cancer. Studies link diets containing large amounts of foods preserved by salting and pickling with an increased risk of stomach, nasopharyngeal, and throat cancer.

Is it true that cooking meat or boiling milk can be harmful?

Cooking and heating is actually necessary to remove harmful germs from meat and milk. However, research suggests that frying, broiling, or grilling meats at very high temperatures creates chemicals that might increase cancer risk. Experts say that the process of pasteurizing milk not only removes germs but also destroys milk's natural enzymes and alters its delicate proteins, causing human-like chronic illnesses and even stillbirth in lab animals.

Does this mean that I shouldn't eat any meat?

It is important to try and keep meat consumption below the recommended 80 to 90 grams as research has

pointed to dangerous effects of consuming too much red meat. Experts advise that it is better to eat fish than red meat.

Are there nutrients that are only existent in animal products and not plant food?

All the nutrients needed to support and enhance our immune functions are readily found in plant foods.

Can fish oil supplements prevent cancer?

So far, research has only shown beneficial effects of Omega-3 fatty acids from natural fish sources. Research has not yet demonstrated any possible benefit from taking fish oil supplements.

What is the link between alcohol and smoking and cancer or heart disease?

Studies have so far indicated that both smoking and regular consumption of alcohol can cause a variety of cancers. A few alcoholic drinks per week can actually increase breast cancer risk in women. The American Cancer Society reports that the combination of alcohol and tobacco increases cancer risk far higher than practicing either habit alone. The American Heart Association warns that smokers' risk of heart attack is more than twice that of non-smokers.

What is the link between too much salt and cancer or heart disease?

The American Cancer Society cautions against consuming foods preserved through the use of salt as these may increase the risk for cancer. The American Heart Association reports that too much salt can lead to high blood pressure which, can in turn, lead to complications like stroke and heart disease. It suggests moderating salt intake to less than 3,000 milligrams a day or about one and a half teaspoons of salt a day.

What is the link between too much sugar and diabetes?

Most people who fear diabetes or already have the disease should be concerned about the glycemic index of a food, not just about the amount of sugar it contains. The glycemic index is the rate at which sugar levels increase in the blood. (For example, glucose has a glycemic index of 100 because if we eat glucose, it raises our blood sugar levels right away.) Most foods eventually turn into glucose, but if we eat rice or bread for instance, it takes longer for our system to turn it into sugar and raise our blood sugar levels.

Generally, the lower the glycemic index, the better it is for diabetics.

Harvesting and processing methods can affect the glycemic index. For example, rice has a different glycemic index depending on how it is processed:

Parboiled rice : 47

Brown rice: 59

White rice : 88

Instant rice: 91 (cooked and dried)

Banana's glycemic index:

Banana picked unripe: 30

Ripe banana: 62

Can I get cancer or heart disease if I am overweight?

The American Cancer Society says that being overweight or obese can increase risk of breast cancer among post-menopausal women and some other cancers such as those of the colon,

gallbladder and kidney. The American Heart Association reports that people who are more than 30% over their ideal body weight are more

201

likely to develop heart disease even if they have no other risk factors like smoking and diabetes. This is because, the extra weight puts a strain on the heart and increases blood pressure and cholesterol.

If I have a genetic risk of cancer, is it too late for me to prevent this?

Cancer is caused when our cells mutate. This risk can either be acquired or hereditary.

Nutrition cannot change our genes. But by eating healthily, we can prevent genetic illnesses from been triggered, help control the illness or reduce the symptoms. The American Cancer Society advises that certain nutrients may protect our cells from mutating or becoming damaged. Physical activity and weight control may also delay or prevent the development of cancer in people with increased genetic risk.

Can consuming many nutrients actually enhance the growth of bacteria or cancer cells?

No, when we eat healthy plant foods, our immune system is boosted. By becoming healthier, it helps us to control the growth of cancer and infections. In fact, when people starve, bacteria and cancer grow even faster because their immune system is not functioning properly and therefore, not able to stop the spread of invaders or mutated cells throughout the body.

How much water and other fluids should I drink?

The American Cancer Society suggests that drinking water and other liquids may reduce the risk of bladder cancer. This is because water dilutes the concentration of carcinogens and shortens

the time in which they are in contact with the bladder lining. Although drinking eight cups of water a day is recommended, the American Journal of Physiology reports that the actual requirement for each individual can differ. Too much water may become burdensome and lead to water intoxication where the kidney cannot keep pace with the fluid intake.

Does "natural" equal "healthy"?

No, not everything natural is healthy.

For example, herbs are divided into food herbs and medicinal herbs. Medicinal herbs cause side effects while food herbs don't. Salicylic acid is a compound isolated from the herb white willow bark to make aspirin. The compound ephedrine, from the herb ephedra, can cause brain hemorrhage in serious cases. Cocaine and tobacco are other examples of natural herbs that can cause harmful side effects. Experts also say that some herbs, although natural, can cause adverse effects when taken with certain prescription or over-the-counter drugs.

Conclusion

Think about how wonderful it would be if you could live to be a 150 years old. Think of all the dreams you could achieve and all the time you would have to visit exotic destinations or watch your great grandkids grow. It is not impossible. Scientists have proven that we have the ability to live that long if we make lifestyle decisions that bolster the immune system.

Good nutrition from natural sources gives us an amazing disease-fighting capability while poor nutrition makes us fall ill easily. When we succumb to chronic illnesses, we age faster. By teaching us about the benefits of plant foods, Nutritional Immunology helps us to strive for longevity and an excellent quality of life.

Nutritional Immunology also focuses on education. Many people fall ill simply because they lack knowledge about nutrition.

It is never too late to embrace the teachings of Nutritional Immunology. Do it today and you could be enjoying a long, full life alongside your great grandchildren.

图书在版编目（CIP）数据

营养免疫学／陈昭妃著. —北京：中国社会出版社，2004.11
ISBN 7-5087-0337-5

Ⅰ.营... Ⅱ.陈... Ⅲ.①营养学－英文②医药学：免疫学－英文
Ⅳ.① R151 ② R392

中国版本图书馆 CIP 数据核字（2004）第 120969 号

书　　名：营养免疫学(英文)

著　　者：陈昭妃

责任编辑：杨春岩

出版发行：中国社会出版社　　　邮编：100032

联通方法：北京市西城区二龙路甲 33 号新龙大厦

　　　　　电话：66051698　　电传：66051713

经　　销：各地新华书店

印刷装订：中国电影出版社印刷厂

开　　本：787×1092 毫米　　　1/16

印　　张：13

版　　次：2004 年 11 月第 1 版

印　　次：2005 年 11 月第 2 次印刷

书　　号：ISBN 7-5087-0337-5/R·44

定　　价：55.00 元

（凡中国社会版图书有缺漏页、残破等质量问题，本社负责调换）